ENDORSEMENTS

About two decades ago, I had the privilege of sitting under the teaching of Jackie Kendall for the first time. The fact that I can remember her message to this day speaks volumes about her gifting. Jackie's signature style of presenting biblical truths with a mix of humor and gut-level honesty has won the trust of many women who find themselves stuck. In her latest work, *Surrender Your Junior God Badge*, Jackie hands over the keys to set women free from the bondage of control and experience the peace their souls crave. You will love this book!

VICKI COURTNEY
Best-selling author of *Rest Assured, Move On,* and
Five Conversations You Must Have With Your Daughter

There are few issues as pervasive and nagging as control, and few people as equipped as Jackie Kendall to address it. The subject of control cloaks itself in sneaky, malicious ways and unless addressed head-on, becomes a distracting, ugly force, marring all relationships, capable of sending our faith-walk into a tailspin. *Surrender Your Junior God Badge* levels a fierce blow to the harrowing spirit of control, and promises to deliver the help, support and wisdom from above that readers of Jackie's books have long enjoyed. I'm ordering ten copies!

DR. STEPHANIE BENNETT
Professor of Communication and author of
Within the Walls Trilogy and *Communicating Love*

From the first time I heard Jackie Kendall speak on the topic of surrendering our counterfeit "Junior God Badges", the mental picture has remained ever present in my daily walk with Christ. Jackie's brutal honesty, extreme transparency and experiential wisdom in breaking down the message of our desire to control struck me on a deeper level than I ever imagined possible, and I'm confident it will do the same for you. Put down your phone, turn off the TV and read this book NOW!

SAMI CONE
Author of *Raising Uncommon Kids* and
host of the nationally-syndicated *Family Money Minute*

I will be buying this book about control for myself and virtually EVERY woman I know. It should just be handed out at the hospital when a girl is born!

SUSIE BETTENHAUSEN
Artist

One of the reasons women are often exhausted is because of the fatiguing nature of trying to control. But, we often blame our fatigue on outside circumstances, such as children, husbands, jobs, family and friends. Jackie poignantly cuts to the heart of the matter—or, rather, the matter of the heart—and articulates most women's fears in a way we feel understood. And by feeling understood, women can read this book and feel encouraged to surrender their "Jr. God Badges"—and their hearts—and rest in the sovereignty of God.

JOY ALLMOND
Writer/Editor, Billy Graham Evangelistic Association,
Freelance Journalist

Life is hard and complicated! Daily, we are tempted to try and fix and control its every detail! My prayer partner for the last 15 years, Jackie Kendall, has prayed me through many of life's painful circumstances, when I tried to control another person's heart to conform to my will, thinking it would make my life easier and less painful. This book, her life message, will encourage the reader in the same way Jackie encouraged me, to surrender all to Jesus because HE IS! He is the Problem Solver, the Omnipotent, Sovereign, All Powerful, All Knowing, the Answer to every need, God. Grab a copy of *Surrender Your Jr. God Badge,* and be prepared to be transformed into the joy-filled woman you have always longed to be.

VICKI ROSE
Author, *Every Reason to Leave*

Ladies, fasten your seatbelt and get ready for the ride of your life! Jackie beautifully and candidly shows us why we as women struggle with control and how we can put away our Jr. God Badge for good. This book has the power to change you and your relationships. Read it! You will never be the same! Bravo Jackie, for sharing these principles that will help us finally "Let It Go!"

DEDE KENDALL
Author, *Wisdom Kids* and *Lady in Waiting for Little Girls*

SURRENDER YOUR JUNIOR GOD BADGE

EVERY WOMAN'S BATTLE
WITH CONTROL

JACKIE KENDALL

DESTINY IMAGE® PUBLISHERS, INC.
P.O. Box 310, Shippensburg, PA 17257-0310
"Promoting Inspired Lives."

This book and all other Destiny Image and Destiny Image Fiction books are available at Christian bookstores and distributors worldwide.

Cover design by Eileen Rockwell
Jr. God Badge design by Andrea Graeve

For more information on foreign distributors, call 717-532-3040.
Or reach us on the Internet: www.destinyimage.com

ISBN 13: TP 978-0-7684-0849-2
ISBN 13 EBook: 978-0-7684-0850-8

For Worldwide Distribution, Printed in the U.S.A.
3 4 5 6 7 8 9 10 11 / 18 17 16

DEDICATION

To Ruth Olsen,
my invaluable life coach and writing mentor

ACKNOWLEDGMENTS

First and foremost, I want to give all praise to my Lord and Savior, Jesus Christ, who has patiently taught me the principles in this book. Jesus has mercifully removed the scales from my eyes in relation to my controlling propensity!

Special thanks to the Destiny Image team that has enthusiastically supported this project. Thank you Ronda Ranalli, John Martin, and Kathryn Deering for your good hearted manner that made working with you a true pleasure.

I want to thank the cheering squad that would not let me quit. I struggled for several years because of the vulnerability this book would require. Several women would not accept any of my excuses and cheered continuously about the need for this book. Joy Allmond led the cheering squad that was composed of DeDe Kendall, Bettye Galbraith, Vicki Rose, and Dr. Stephanie Bennett.

I am thankful for my two adult children, Ben and Jessica, whom God has used to expose my deep need of surrendering my Junior God Badge.

Last but not least, my husband Ken, who has patiently loved me for forty years even though I was a recovering control freak!

CONTENTS

SURRENDER YOUR JUNIOR GOD BADGE

Lots of people wear badges. Police and firefighters have the shiny bronze ones; soldiers are given a badge of honor for courage and valor; Girl Scouts work hard to fill up their sashes with merit badges. A badge can be a token of membership to a group or a cause, like those little lapel pins for the Elks or Lions Club or even a political campaign button. A badge is a way of announcing to the world, "This is who I am. This is what I stand for. This is what I've accomplished." Sometimes we earn a badge and it's bestowed upon us, and sometimes we choose to pin a statement on ourselves.

The common theme about badges is that they display something important about our identity—and something that's legitimately true. You wouldn't pick up the Fire Chief's badge and lead the brigade to the flames. You wouldn't wear your grandfather's Purple Heart medal and boast about your patriotic bravery. Badges mean something because they're authentic.

This is a book about a very particular badge. And here's the thing about it: It's a counterfeit. This is the badge that all of us own and none of us earned—the *Junior God Badge*.

For more than two decades I have taught about this counterfeit Junior God Badge. This book has grown organically during my teaching of "Surrender Your Junior God Badge" throughout the United States. I have been teaching for almost forty years, and the *one message* women always refer back to is the one about the "Junior God Badge."

TAKING OVER GOD'S JOB DESCRIPTION

Whether you are married, divorced, single, or widowed—all you need to be controlling is your pulse as a woman. I had been studying the names of God and His characteristics, and the thought came to me: "Women try to do this all the time!" We try to be the Alpha and the Omega. We think that we're the One who provides (*Jehovah Jirah*) and the One who heals (*Jehovah Rapha*), the Wonderful Counselor and the Way, the Truth, and the Life. As I began to recognize this reality, the Lord graciously gave me an encouraging "correction" by revealing to me the core issue of my soul. I wore a "Junior God Badge." And like a sheriff who takes his badge *very* seriously, who wears it with pride and functions out of its authority, this Junior God Badge absolutely defined me. I began to realize that I was trying to "be God" in all kinds of situations, and that badge was the daily reminder of my role. Having that badge securely in place, I would feel pretty confident that I would be the woman of my husband's dreams and the joy of my children's heart and the most awesome child of the King!

Now, you may be thinking already, "What is wrong with wanting to be the best wife, mother, and child of the King?" My answer—nothing is wrong with wanting to be the best. But what is the *motivation* behind that noble desire? What are the *methods* we use to bring it about? This is what God wanted me to see. He wanted me to see that I was taking over *His* job description!

Before long, I began to teach about the common qualities of a Junior God Badge owner. I had a prayer partner at that time, who was gifted and skilled in crafts; and after hearing me speak on this topic, she made me an elaborate Junior God Badge. It was as large as a bread plate, painted gold and backed with lace. The words "Junior God Badge" were emblazoned on it in silver glitter. When she first showed it to me, I thought, "I can't wear that huge thing!" But just as quickly as I recoiled from it, I realized it was perfect. My control issues were so *big* and so *gaudy* that they caught the attention, not only of God, but of everyone around me. So what did I do? I purchased a large chain to mount the badge on, and I wore it whenever I taught "Surrender Your Junior God Badge."

Since being awakened to this fact all those years ago, I have learned that if you are a female older than twelve and still have breath in your body, you live with the DNA of the original controlling woman—Eve. In the chapters to come, we will examine closely the reality that we are all little Eves—Evettes! The controlling woman strives daily to perfect God-like qualities in her life. They may seem impressive, but they are ultimately a vain attempt to tame the untamable and to avoid suffering. This Junior God Badge owner is a woman who is a "wannabe deity."

THE SEED THAT GREW INTO A TREE OF SURRENDER

Let me share with you the simple devotional I wrote all those years ago that became the seed for my lessons on this topic and, ultimately, this book:

> Where did this "Junior God Badge" originate? Who was the first person who struggled with the desire to run the universe, or at least his or her part of the planet? I don't mean to pick on our dear mother, Eve, but she was the first woman who decided that control was better than dependence on God. Now, she was not the first "being" that wanted the Junior God title—that belongs to Lucifer, whose "love song" of independence (see Isa. 14:12-15) transported him from heaven to hell. Now he roams planet Earth in an attempt to enlist people in his choir!
>
> This Junior God Badge mentality manifests itself in the basic need to control. The woman with this propensity will actually feel the responsibility of living out the very characteristics of God.

I know this woman very well, and I have experienced all her propensities.

For example, the omnipresent woman can be found zooming through the day, rushing here and there to be everything to everybody. She is doing her best to be everywhere for everyone so that she can keep everyone in her world happy. This omnipresent woman ends up frustrated and fatigued.

The omnipotent woman has unrealistic, grandiose expectations of herself. Common phrases used by her throughout the day are: "I can do it. I'll get it. I'll fix it. I'll do it." She is so driven to make everyone happy that she even worries about God's needs.

The omniscient woman is driven by the need to be all-knowing (constantly reading, attending seminars) so she can use her knowledge to control, pressure, and manipulate those in her world. Controlling them for their good is her reason—but also her blind spot.

The sovereign woman manifests the heart of the need to control. "I am in charge so no one will get hurt." She is afraid to surrender the terrible burden she is carrying—the burden of always wanting life on her terms.

Only God Almighty can be all-knowing, all-powerful, and always present—never fatigued, frustrated, drained, aggravated, or burned out. Wow, I am already tired and it is only 2:07 P.M.!

I think I am going to remove my Junior God Badge and put it back in the junk drawer in my kitchen. The Lord has given me the freedom to wear the badge—if I want to burn out myself and others. Once again, I choose to remove my Junior God Badge, pour myself a Diet Coke, and let God be in charge; I am just too tired.

For anyone who enters God's rest also rests from his own work, just as God did from His (Heb. 4:10).[1]

This book is the tree that grew from this seed of a thought. May the branches of this tree provide a shady place where you can sit and find peace from your exhausted life of trying in vain to control an uncontrollable world. Come join me now in this cool, refreshing place beneath the Tree of Surrender rather than the Tree of the Knowledge of Good and Evil that got the original Eve into the mess we are still trying to sanitize!

Note: In August, 2012, I sent that devotional "seed" to hundreds of friends with the following request: *Big favor, please: Would you consider contributing your thoughts to my next book? How can you contribute? After reading this devotional, would you please email me your thoughts about a woman's struggle with "control?" I would be so grateful for your input.*

I am so grateful for many of their thoughtful replies now quoted throughout this book.

WHEN PLAN B IS YOUR PLAN A

Years ago I ran across this poem, "Life Is All About How You Handle Plan B":

> *Plan A is always my first choice.*
> *You know, the one where*
> *Everything works out to be*
> *Happily ever after.*
> *But more often than not,*
> *I find myself dealing with*
> *The upside-down, inside-out version—*
> *Where nothing goes as it should.*
> *It's at this point that the real*
> *Test of my character comes in.*
> *Do I sink, or do I swim?*
> *Do I wallow in self-pity and play the victim,*
> *Or simply shift gears*
> *And make the best of the situation?*
> *The choice is all mine...*
> *Life is all about how you handle Plan B.*[2]

Perfectly reflecting the spirit of this poem is a letter I received from another (beloved) control freak. The summary of her letter actually declares that in God's sovereignty, what looks like Plan B is actually Plan A. Enjoy the letter. (Thanks Jessica Wuerffel!)

In 2005, I had the fortune of experiencing Hurricane Katrina firsthand. I realize that "fortune" is not the word most would think of regarding the act of losing your home and seeing your entire city flooded. For me, however, the lessons I learned from that experience far outweighed my material loss.

You see, I am a control freak. There. I said it.

I like order, predictability, stability, and the opportunity to manipulate my circumstances at will. I shy away from chaos, impulsivity, and schedule changes.

That is where God comes in. Just when I think I have everything under control, He likes to rip the rug out from under me. Though unpleasant, losing my footing is a great reminder of Who is actually in control. And, honey, that isn't me!

At the start of August 2005, my husband and I, our 20-month old son, and our dog were living in the Lakeview section of New Orleans. Our work, Desire Street Ministries, was located in the upper ninth ward. Late in the month, we noticed a disturbance brewing in the Gulf of Mexico. Soon enough, a monster was born.

We were at first encouraged, and then told, to evacuate as quickly as possible. So we packed up our car with our insurance papers, the dog's cage, a few pictures, four changes of clothes each, a bit of food, and some odds and ends. Within 48 hours, that was all we owned. Katrina had split open the Industrial Canal, wiping away the ministry, as well as the 17th Street Canal, wiping away our home.

Losing our home was not in my "perfect planning." It wasn't on my schedule for that Tuesday, so how dare it occur?

In our home, we refer to our days as abiding by either Plan A or Plan B. Plan B is the one we design. Plan A operates by God's perfect design. Plan A is often more chaotic because, well, we did not plan on it, but the results are far sweeter.

Hurricane Katrina was God's Plan A. It afforded me the opportunity to see majesty at work. To see direction directed. To see order in chaos. And more than anything, it afforded me the opportunity to let go. Watching God orchestrate the wind and the rain was a clear reminder that I am *not* in control, no matter how much order I attempt to orchestrate.

There is a great freedom in letting go. Freedom in not having to make sure everything is "just so." Freedom in not creating a schedule. Freedom to be. Freedom to float. Freedom to let go and let God. Praise God for Plan A.[3]

A MESSIAH FOR MY FAMILY

What I am going to share next, I was going to place at the *end* of this book, but my husband suggested that I share it as you and I begin this journey together. I am going to share my *biggest regret* as a controlling woman.

This one is so painful that I am actually nauseated as I type, but I know people are liberated when the candid vulnerability of others shows them that they are not alone in their failure, struggles, and shattered dreams, so here I go—my heart in print.

My greatest regret is spending four decades trying to rescue my family of origin from destructive behavior. I have spent *so* much time and *so* much money trying to "save them" from *so* many poor choices. You might think that my tenacity is commendable, but the hard truth is that my tenacity was not led by God—it was compelled by my stubborn, controlling self. I have spent four desperate decades diligently wearing my Junior God Badge, sacrificing countless hours of effort and worry and heartache trying to drag my family away from destructive behavior. *Not one* of my family members has been "saved" from their destructive patterns! I will not share the details of the day that the scales on my eyes were removed—except to say that I wept so hard I could have vomited up my organs. I kept repeating, "I could have sent thousands of Bibles to India and China with the money that I wasted on people who love their addictions more than God." My passion to be my family's messiah was not good.

You would think that after the suicide of *two* siblings I would realize how powerless I am over my siblings—but the suicides actually became my motivation to get a "PhD in Control." After paying for yet another stint in rehab, when a particular sibling relapsed again, I drove, weeping, to an Al-Anon meeting. That night I heard a 70-year-old man tell of the heartache his son was still putting him through, and I just gasped. I seriously thought I could not breathe. But the Lord used that man's remarks to throw a bucket of ice water in my face. That night the scales on my eyes were beginning to peel off. The final surgery was in our kitchen when I heard the painful truth of the vanity of my controlling efforts—not from a professional counselor or my pastor, but from my oldest child! It is pretty sad when you, the adult, have to hear the truth from your child.

Surrender Your Junior God Badge addresses our counterfeit authority to do what cannot be done—but what every woman *thinks* she can do—control another person's heart. "The heart is deceitful above all things and beyond cure. Who can understand it? 'I the Lord search the heart and examine the mind, to reward each person according to their conduct, according to what their deeds deserve'" (Jer. 17:9-10).

Controllers with their Junior God Badges pinned to their shirts assume they know how to change the hearts of those they love. Ironically, though, the Word clearly states that the controller's heart is as deceitful as those she is trying to change!

SHAKING THE UNSHAKABLE

When I was a young woman, I had so much "God-confidence" that one would wonder if I weren't really a little arrogant. Honestly, my daily reading of God's Word would infuse such hope and joy into my soul that I went about life with a passionate focus, and I was always surprised that people considered such passion unique.

One of my God-confident building moments came when I was invited to speak at a large women's event in Oklahoma, and they wanted to know how to "define me" for the brochure; I should mention that the roster of speakers included none other than Miss Oklahoma. As I struggled with how to spice up a "stay at home mom" bio, I read the following verse: "Since we are receiving a Kingdom that is unshakable, let us be thankful and please God by worshipping Him with holy fear and awe (Heb. 12:28, NLT). Instantly this phrase came to my heart and mind, "Jackie, you are a princess from an *unshakable Kingdom*." Later that day, I called the event director and gave her my description. She chuckled at first, and then I quoted the source of my God-confidence and she said, "That is wonderful."

As the years passed, my life became more complex, and instead of relying on the fact that I serve a God of an unshakable Kingdom and I am His princess, I began to cling to my Junior God Badge. Increasingly, I was depending on *my* lists and *my* blueprints and *my* scripts as the roadmaps for life. But then my confidence began to be shaken. The very plans I thought were "unshakable" were being shaken by my attempts to control the chaos around me. My driven intent to control caused me to forfeit my God-confidence, and the princess from an unshakable Kingdom was stumbling all around in desperation, trying to control the uncontrollable.

In the following pages, I will share with you glimpses of how my confidence in Papa God and His unshakable Kingdom was restored. I now have learned not to dread when the ground beneath my feet begins to quake. And it all begins and ends with one act of faith: Surrender.

DISCLAIMER: WOMEN ARE NOT THE ONLY CONTROLLERS

"How to Know if You Are a Controlling Person." The moment I saw this title in a blog by Donald Miller, I knew I had to include it so that women would not think they are being called out as the only exclusive club of controllers. *Insecurity* allows control to be an equal-opportunity style of life, whether you are male or female!

This book will focus on control in a woman's life, but I want to state upfront that control is an issue for all human beings. In fact, a very insightful blog post by a guy exposes the source of control in everyone's life. The following excerpt is from that blog, and Donald Miller's vulnerability exposes a great picture of the insecurity that fuels our control.

> I realized I was a controlling person not long ago when a therapist caught me in the act. I was wondering out loud why a friend was doing what she was doing, and the therapist questioned why I was trying to get inside somebody else's head. "What does it matter why people do what they do? Are you trying to predict behavior to gain a sense of security?"

It was a terrific observation. Trying to figure out why people are doing what they are doing is a preface to trying to control or influence them indirectly. If I really wanted to know why they were doing what they were doing, I could just ask. But I didn't want to ask because it was none of my business. They had a right to think and do as they wished.

Here are a few ways to know whether you might be a controlling person:

- You imagine a life in which somebody else was different, and indirectly try to affect their change.

- You get angry when things aren't going your way and you let people know it.

- You can only be surrounded by people who are submissive to you.

- You give the silent treatment to people you are angry with.

- You are often tempted to show people the errors they don't see in themselves.[4]

CHAPTER 1

ORIGIN: THE ORIGINAL PATENT FOR THE JUNIOR GOD BADGE

We see exhausted, frazzled women everywhere we go. Why are we all so exhausted so often? You may think of a thousand reasons, but I am convinced that the most common reason that all women from all walks of life are stressed out, and worn out is their propensity to try to be the Head Chick in Charge. Trying to be in charge in an out-of-control world inevitably leads to exhaustion.

On a woman's best day, the illusion of control has her in a trance. For a brief moment, she feels "large and in charge," and life is good. Her badge is on. She may even have that Life is Good decal on her car—evidence that the illusion of control is captivating, yet another descendant of Eve. This woman needs to be pulled over and issued a ticket for wearing that infamous Junior God Badge! But, you know what? She doesn't even know she has the badge on. She automatically removes it at night when she goes to sleep, and she puts it on a fresh outfit when she wakes up in the morning. Wearing this controlling badge of honor is as natural for a woman as breathing. Where did she get this Junior God Badge?

EVETTE DNA: LEGACY HEIRLOOM

We females, women and girls alike, are all little Evettes. The Mother of the human race, Eve, was the original owner of the Junior God Badge; and like a good mama, she bequeathed us a precious family heirloom that has now been passed down from generation to generation. Let's look at the passage that shows how the first Junior God Badge was created: "Unto the woman He said, I will greatly multiply thy sorrow and thy conception; in sorrow thou shalt bring forth children; and thy desire shall be to thy husband, and he shall rule over thee" (Gen. 3:16, KJV).

Because this verse is a key to understanding where all this desire to control flowed from, I asked a dear friend, Courtney Veasey, who is working on her doctorate at New Orleans Baptist Theological Seminary, if she could send me a literal translation of Genesis 3:16. Here is what she sent:

> To the woman He said, "Increasing I will increase [which means "I will certainly make to increase/ or increase greatly"] your anxious toil [same word in the curse on Adam in Genesis 3:17) and your pregnancy. With strenuous work (hurt) you will

bear children and to/for your husband you will desire (overflow with yearning, longing, desire) and he will rule over you." (*Rule* is used in Genesis 1:16 and 18, and it's used often in reference to kings, too.)

I am not trying to write an exegetical treatise on the ramifications of this passage, but I do want you, as a woman, to understand that the DNA of a woman's anxiety and her need to control is something *she arrived with* when she took her first breath. The second chapter of this book will address in great detail the words "increase greatly your anxious toil." These words concern a woman's default setting on anxiety. In this chapter, however, I will address the final part of this Scripture regarding a woman's overflowing desire for her "ruling" husband.

For too many years I misunderstood "her desire shall be for her husband," because I thought it referred to her romantic heartbeat for her man. In college, my professor quoted Lord Byron one time, and I never forgot the phrase: "To a woman, love is her whole life, to a man, only a part of his life." So I always assumed that this imbalance in love was part of the curse of Eve in chapter three of Genesis. The poet Ella Wheeler Wilcox (1850–1919) wrote:

> *It ever has been since time began,*
> *And ever will be, till time lose breath,*
> *That love is a mood—no more—to a man,*
> *And love to a woman is life or death.*[5]

Did Lord Byron and Ella Wheeler Wilcox capture the meaning of these verses? For years I was satisfied with these descriptions, but then, when I looked a little closer at the context, I began to see something else. Perhaps this part of the curse of Eve was more than just unrequited love. As I looked at a Hebrew Lexicon and read the phrase about overflowing desire, I began to ponder that the desire might not be simply for her "ruling" husband.[6] When you put the translated words back in context, you see that she has the overflowing desire of something she wants, *but* her husband has the rule, like a king. The words, "overflowing desire" actually collide with the word, "rule," and what's being depicted here is really a conflict of interest. A precious brother in Jesus once described that conflict of interest like this: "Eve's overflowing desire wanted to bypass her hubby's dominion with her own agenda and intent."

AN OVERFLOWING DESIRE TO CONTROL

When I think of the origin of that Junior God Badge, I think of the moment in Scripture when it actually comes into play for the first time. (Of course the badge was not immediately pinned to fig leaves or animal skins, but it appeared on the heart attitude!). Here's the place: "Then the woman saw that the tree was good for food and delightful to look at, and that it was desirable for obtaining wisdom. So she took some of its fruit and ate it; she also gave some to her husband who was with her, and he ate it" (Gen. 3:6, HCSB).

Forty-nine words that changed life forever—not only for Eve and her Adam, but for all the Evettes who would ever be born. Eve gave the fruit to her hubby to eat, and eat he did! Talk about a controlling woman and a man who submitted to her controlling influence! For many years when I read this verse I wondered, *Why didn't Adam yell, "Don't touch the tree, Eve!"?* Then I read *The Silence of Adam* by Dr. Larry Crabb. Writing about this passage in Genesis 3:6, Dr. Crabb's observation is that at the very moment of choice, Eve was controlling and Adam was a coward. I was overwhelmed by his remark, pondering it for a long time.

It's true. Through the centuries this situation has continued—controlling women and cowardly men. We see it in our churches. John Maxwell once said, "Eighty percent of the work being done in the local church is done by women." Women often justify their work and control because too often they have experienced the apathy and cowardice of men. In fact, I have experienced this so many times that I could write an entire separate book on what I have observed. Let it be enough to comment about the many times in couples' Bible studies when wise and gifted men do not speak up. One time I asked my husband why the men tended to stay silent. His immediate reply was, "They don't need to talk, because the women will *gladly* answer the discussion questions." I asked an elder who was attending our home Bible study why he didn't speak up that much. He replied, "Well, sometimes I am not sure that my answer is correct, so I don't want to look stupid in front of my friends." *Really*?

THE FIRST WOMEN'S LIBBER

Let's just take a moment and clarify that Gloria Steinem was not the original leader of the Women's Liberation Movement—and neither was Elizabeth Cady Stanton, or Joan of Arc. The first woman who thought she was smarter than God and the man He created was *Eve*. Eve exchanged dependence on the Creator of the Universe for independence and a life of untamable chaos and heartache. Way to go, Eve! The serpent deceived Eve into thinking that control was better than dependence: "For God knows that when you eat from it your eyes will be opened, and you will be like God, knowing good and evil" (Gen. 3:5).

Eve ate the forbidden fruit because she wanted to be more like God, and we are still eating that fruit today. For every owner of a Junior God Badge, wanting to be like God is the foundation for living. Daily, our lives declare our dependence or independence.

A young woman named Megan Bartnick responded to my invitation to share about being controlling:

> I noticed your post about a woman's struggle with "control." I'm only 20, and my input probably doesn't mean as much. However, control is a big struggle of mine. I often find that I struggle with control, because the more I feel in control the more I feel secure. It's a struggle to allow God to be in control, because I do not know what's going

to happen, and I have no way of directing what will happen. My job is to trust, obey, pray, and wait. I also know the plans I want to carry out and the desires of my heart that I want fulfilled. I get the silly idea that I know best how to carry out those plans and fulfill those desires. I have to go to God's Word and remind myself that God can do far more than I could ask or imagine (see Ephesians 3:20), and He has a special plan for me (see Jeremiah 29:11). It's a constant, daily struggle to let go of control, but this struggle always brings me to the feet of Jesus.

Some women protest when I quote the curse in Genesis 3:16, because they believe that they are no longer under the curse. Boldly, they will tell me that the curse was removed by Jesus hanging on the cross. My reply, "So Jesus removed the curse, then what about pain in childbirth?"

Now I do know a couple of women who got drugs early in the delivery process so they were throwing a party during labor. Drugs can now take the edge off of the pain of childbirth, but labor is not the only pain that a child brings a woman!

CONTROL AND OUR DNA

When I first start speaking on the Junior God Badge, it is not unusual for part of the audience to start thinking of a friend or relative who is controlling. And it's not only quiet, submissive women who assume that they do not have a problem with control; some boisterous and assertive women merely see themselves as good leaders and great organizers. Furthermore, the sophisticated southern belle would gasp at the suggestion that she was controlling. But let me tell you a secret: Southern charm is often a very effective disguise for *control*. Sweet whining (think Scarlet O'Hara in *Gone with the Wind*) has worked on many men, except Captain Rhett Butler. Scarlett O'Hara would never have admitted that she was manipulative and controlling. When Rhett Butler came into her life, she refused to own her agenda, and it ultimately cost her everything.

While Scarlett is a big personality, control is actually not based on personality (although personality certainly affects what control looks like, whether it's obvious or subtle). Control is simply part of our DNA, and it's called *the flesh*. We're all Evettes. If I asked your family or fellow workers if you are controlling, they would all say yes (well, at least the honest ones would.) Whenever I have mentioned that I am writing a book on women and their controlling tendency, rarely do women say, "I need that book for my friend." They know they need it for themselves. Most women are humble enough to admit it, and once they learn about the Junior God Badge, they will also admit to having a whole collection of them that match their outfits!

One doctor's wife from Boca Raton jokingly remarked, "I have my Junior God Badges all color-coordinated!" Another godly woman, Letha Crouch, wrote in an email about her many Junior God Badges, "I have holes in all my outfits [from pinning them on], like I'm always dressed in eyelet material!" I have had the privilege of meeting controlling women all over the United States, and they all have the characteristics of Eve, their original mom. I am thinking of a woman who has the softest voice, but who is the most controlling woman I have ever met. She gets away with manipulation and control because people are absolutely hypnotized by her syrupy sweet tone.

AN EVERGREEN TREE OR A STUNTED SHRUB?

This is what the Lord says: "Cursed are those who put their trust in mere humans, who rely on human strength and turn their hearts away from the Lord. They are like stunted shrubs in the desert, with no hope for the future. They will live in the barren wilderness, in an uninhabited salty land.

"But blessed are those who trust in the Lord and have made the Lord their hope and confidence. They are like trees planted along a riverbank, with roots that reach deep into the water. Such trees are not bothered by the heat or worried by long months of drought. Their leaves stay green, and they never stop producing fruit" (Jer. 17:5-8, NLT).

My dependence on God allows me to be ever green and ever fruitful, but my independence from God results in my being a hopeless stunted shrub. When I surrender my Junior God Badge and return to dependence on God,

I can end the stunted shrub condition and become ever so fruitful.

Barbara Sullivan, author of *The Control Trap*, was speaking at a national conference when she captured with one remark the perfect description of being such a hopeless, stunted shrub. Barbara said, "Control is an outgrowth of *fear, insecurity and lack of self-esteem*. The more anxious a woman is, the more she wants to control. Conversely, the more secure a woman is, the less likely she will need to control."

Fear, insecurity, lack of self-esteem, and anxiety—we will address these suffocating qualities in chapter 2, but it's worth seeing these characteristics in light of the prophet Jeremiah's description of life in the barren wilderness.

COMMON BLIND SPOT FOR ALL EVETTES

A common self-deception for all Evettes is the expectation that she can change the one she loves. Desiring to change the object of one's desire begins early, and it continues until a woman learns that only God can change another human being. This is one reason that girls use to justify dating a non-believer. Girls think they are smarter than God and that they will be able to transform the object of their love and desire through their great influence and wisdom.

My sister-in-law, DeDe, shared about teaching ninth-graders some of the principles from my book, *Lady in Waiting*. The class was composed of both guys and girls. She passed out the following list and asked the students to follow the directions at the top:

Put a check beside each of the following characteristics *that you can change* in your spouse after marriage:

- Unwillingness to communicate
- Dominating ego
- Bad temper
- Argumentative tendencies
- Difficulty in apologizing
- Bad language
- Unwillingness to be in involved with church
- Inability to keep a job
- Jealousy
- Self-centeredness
- Depression
- Unwillingness to give
- Wandering eyes
- Lying
- Immaturity
- Workaholic tendencies

DeDe watched in amazement as the girls busily checked items on the list. She noticed that the boys had not checked *any* items on their lists. When asked why they didn't check anything, several boys spoke up saying, "I can't change another person's behavior." Here were ninth-grade boys who knew this already. The girls in the class were surprised at the boys' comments and began to argue about a person's capacity to change the object of their love. DeDe laughed as she listened to the girls defend their power to change someone and the boys' response—"No way!"

The girls are junior Evettes already. My favorite story about a junior Evette was given to me by the father of my daughter's best junior high school friend. This wonderful man was driving a bunch of kids home from church, including my daughter, when the van blew a tire. What this man didn't know was that he had a bigger problem than a flat tire. In his van, was a junior Evette who was about to blow a fuse, because the delay in getting home was just not tolerable. This little Evette had a champion controller for a mom—*me!*

Yes. My daughter Jessi got out of the van with the rest of the kids, but she didn't stay with the kids. Jessi walked over to Mr. Bonner, who was bent over, changing the tire, and asked: "How long is this going to take?" He must have been stunned, sweating in the Florida humidity in his dress suit.

Mr. Bonner replied, "Why?"

Jessi, hands on hips, tapping her toe, was all huffy that *her* schedule had been derailed by a flat tire. "I need to get home and finish my homework!"

Let me reiterate: If you are a woman older than twelve and you're breathing, you have an issue with control. This is true even though I have had many a young woman tell me that I was describing her mother when she heard this teaching. Ironically she only sees it as her mother's issue, although it is also her issue.

Why worry about a speck in your friend's eye when you have a log in your own? (See Matthew 7:3-4.) Here's something to consider—making a "holy habit": The next time you see a controlling moment in another woman's life, pray not only for her, *but also for yourself.*

DYSFUNCTIONAL SENSE OF RESPONSIBILITY

Women of all ages and stages of life are constantly searching for the means to change those they love. This often desperate attempt to change others is fueled by a dysfunctional sense of responsibility. Controlling women think they are responsible to change people who are not going in the right direction.

Ironically, there are support groups all across our nation that exist to help men and women who are at the end of their ropes in attempting to make another person change. The very first step of those programs states, "We came to believe we were *powerless* over other people." "Powerless" doesn't mean "victim," but rather it means that this dysfunctional sense of responsibility will not end until a woman, young or old, surrenders her Junior God Badge to God Himself. Only God can change a person's interior.

A "deceived controller" is trying to change a "deceitful heart" in another person! This is almost the ultimate irony! (See Jeremiah 17:9-10.)

SEEKING IMMUNIZATION AGAINST SUFFERING

For years I have been aware of my fear-filled propensity to dodge suffering at all cost. What I didn't realize was that my intent to avoid pain was costing me emotionally and spiritually. It took one person quoting one statement to reveal to me my own self-harming behavior. Here's what happened...

More than a decade ago, I was a speaker for a Pro-Athletes Outreach (PAO) Conference in West Palm Beach, Florida. One of the other speakers for the conference was Pastor Steve Brown. I was excited about hearing Pastor Brown that evening, because I had listened to him on Christian radio for years, and I couldn't wait to hear what he had for us at this conference. His message began with one statement, and I did not hear another thing the rest of the night. Here is the life-impacting remark:

> *The source of all emotional and spiritual ills is an inappropriate effort to avoid pain.*

Pause right now and reread that sentence.

I looked around the room after writing down the comment, searching for someone as "bowled over" as I was. After the session I asked a couple of people about the remark, and they didn't even remember the statement. Well, for this Master of Control, it was a nuclear blast to my soul. This book is my heart's confession of the serious emotional and spiritual ills I have experienced trying to avoid pain and to control the universe for myself and those I so love.

I controlled because I didn't want pain to come into the lives of those I love. In trying to make all the circumstances for those we love *just right*, I'd obsess over holidays, birthdays and family vacations, trying to get all of my ducks in a perfect row because I was so afraid that something was going to go wrong. I was familiar with the daily internal dialogue: "But what if _____ doesn't come to our holiday celebration? ...But someone might ruin the birthday surprise. ...But what if our flight is delayed and we miss the connection and the special gathering we're trying to get to? ...But we'll look stupid if we arrive just as people are leaving!"

The common element within this anxious fretting? This internal dialogue is full of the conjunction "but," which I call the "conjunction of dysfunction." This conjunction has *no faith* in our sovereign God. This conjunction produces incomprehensible levels of fearful torment. And yet, in God's characteristic fashion, He takes this conjunction of dysfunction, *but,* and turns it into the very pivot-point of hope for us. In chapter 2 of the letter to the Hebrews, we're told that God has put *all* things under the subjection or control of Jesus (verse 8). We may not yet *see* all things under His control (hence *our* attempts to control things ourselves). Then comes the first word in verse 9—*but*..."But we see Jesus..." This transforms our anxious "conjunction of dysfunction" to look at Jesus and to know, from God's Word, that He is in control of all things! So the next time you hear yourself saying, "But what if...? But she can't.... But I have to...," do a grammatical intervention on yourself and change that to God's version of the conjunction: *But we see Jesus....*

Another reason for holding onto this delusional goal of immunizing ourselves against pain and suffering is the assumption that being really deep spiritually means you're immune to real suffering. That's a lie. Being close to Jesus does not grant anyone immunity from disappointment. Consider one who was very close to Him, John the Baptist. Was he protected from disappointment and suffering? Here's someone who was linked with Jesus from before birth, one about whom Jesus said, "none greater than John the Baptist has appeared" (see Matthew 11:11), and yet he suffered imprisonment, disappointment, and, in the end, beheading. No, far from being immune from suffering, it's part of the life of one who follows the Son of God: "everyone who wants to live a godly life in Christ Jesus will suffer persecution" (2 Tim. 3:12, NLT).

I have seen so many Christians become disappointed with God when they are facing unimaginable circumstances. Circumstances beyond one's control are the ultimate suffering for the controlling woman. The Junior God Badge owner is terrified when she is staring down circumstances that she can do absolutely nothing about. And at the crux of that terror is the assumption that she is immune to disappointment with God—assuming her faith and wisdom and depth and strength can keep her from such a fragile state. Controlling women actually fall apart when God doesn't do what she expects Him to do. How do I know that is true? Because it has happened so many times to me and those other controlling women I know and love. Just like John the Baptist, a controlling woman becomes disappointed with God when God doesn't do what she expects Him to do.

John the Baptist was doubting and offended because Jesus had not done what the Scriptures had declared the Messiah would do: "The Spirit of the Lord God is on Me, because the Lord has anointed Me to bring good news to the poor. He has sent Me to heal the brokenhearted, to proclaim liberty to the captives, and *freedom to the prisoners*" (Isa. 61:1-2, HCSB emphasis added).

CONTROLLING WOMEN AND BLURRED VISION

Controlling women are inclined to assume that their spiritual competency not only fortifies them against suffering but also protects them from the vulnerability of doubt and disappointment with God. But the key to facing difficult circumstances is not rushing to get a vaccination against disappointment and pain; it is rushing to the throne of God's grace and counting on Him to sustain you. This is true whether you are in a prison cell facing death or a hospital hallway waiting for the doctor or in a court room waiting for a judge.

For the dependent woman, God's grace is available. For the independent woman, it's a different story. Unfortunately, the independent Junior God Badge wearer thinks she is Wonder Woman and that she can soar beyond the reach of human disappointment and suffering. This means that the independent, controlling woman is often not a candidate for the grace of God. Why is this? Because God only gives grace to the humble (who have been knocked down by circumstances) and He resists (keeps at a distance) the proud (see James 4:5-6). This book is meant to expose the grace-resistant condition of the Junior God Badge wearer in her incessant striving to tame an untamable world.

Are you a grace-resistant woman? Or have you experienced the privilege of having an unimaginable capacity to face the unimaginable?

DISCUSSION QUESTIONS

1. What do you think about the Evette DNA—the Legacy Heirloom of Control? (See Genesis 3:16.)

2. Do you see yourself as a woman with an overflowing desire to control? Or are you thinking about another woman when considering this question? Explain what you are coming to understand. (See Genesis 3:6.)

3. Take a moment to discuss the following quote: "Control is an outgrowth of fear, insecurity and lack of self-esteem. The more anxious a woman is the more she wants to control and conversely, the more secure a woman is the less likely she will need to control" (Barbara Sullivan). Are you surprised that control flows from fear, insecurity and lack of self-esteem? (See Psalm 139:14.)

4. Do you know a woman who has a dysfunctional sense of responsibility? Is the woman you? What's next, after you see what's happening? (See Galatians 6:2,5.)

5. Spend a few moments discussing this quote: "The source of all emotional and spiritual ills is an inappropriate effort to avoid pain" (Steve Brown). (See 2 Corinthians 12:9-10.)

6. Here are a few ways to know whether you might be a controlling person (from Donald Miller):

- You imagine a life in which somebody else was different, and indirectly try to affect their change.

- You get angry when things aren't going your way and you let people know it.

- You can only be surrounded by people who are submissive to you.

- You give the silent treatment to people you are angry with.

- You are often tempted to show people the errors they don't see in themselves

7. With the study group (if you are reading this book together with others), share your own example of controlling behavior.

CHAPTER 2

CONTROL FUELED BY FEAR

Jacquelyn Ezzo shares her experience in overcoming fear and anxiety:

> That relentless sense of urgency to want to control woke me up at 1:39 this morning. This sense expresses its own thoughts and ways that I can make people see and do things my way! Over and over, playing scenario after scenario in my head of how it will go down, what I will say, what they will say, etc., etc...
>
> I toss and turn and try to shut it up—shut it off, pray it away—only to be left irritated, tired and trying to get back to sleep.
>
> As I awake, I find that the sense is still there, only it's a more anxious, panicky feeling of being unsure of how I will respond to this morning's

demands and scenarios, and whether or not I will be able to keep my mouth shut this a.m. and not respond negatively. In my awake reality I am purposely trying to not respond angrily and just pass along information to the person who is supposed to be responsible. I even want to control that. Of course, most of the time nothing is done with the information given, and in my sick way of thinking I say no one will pay for their indiscretion. No one, of course, but me. I pay. I pay with insomnia, anxiety, insanity, anger, vengefulness, unforgiveness, and no peace. I have a choice, though. A choice to continue this way or to walk away. To surrender. To seek and find.

So this morning I went seeking. Lovingly and calmly and so peacefully, Jesus leads me to this devotion: "rest in my loving gaze and you will receive deep peace." *Yes!* That is what I want! Deep peace! Not the momentary peace this world gives me, but the deep peace that resides so deep into my being that only Jesus could put it there. So today I am choosing that deep peace that only He can give through seeking, asking and finding!

Jacquelyn, like many others, is a "wannabe deity." At least she knows what to do about it! Before we examine the ways a controlling woman is a wannabe deity, we need to expose the motive behind her behavior. The rest of this book will be showing the wannabe deity in her daily activities. However, before we examine where control is "camouflaged," we need to consider the deep core of control—and it is not strength—it is *fear*. Let's review Barbara Sullivan's quote from the first chapter that called out fear, insecurity, lack of self-esteem, and anxiety: "Control is an outgrowth of fear, insecurity and lack of self-esteem. The more anxious a woman is the more she wants to control, and conversely, the more secure a woman is the less likely she will need to control."

Those four states of mind are what fuel our desire to control. In this chapter we will primarily address *fear*, because fear is a core motive behind a woman's insecurity and lack of self-esteem, which in turn breed anxiety.

You may recall the theme of anxiety from Genesis 3:16. A critical phrase in the "curse of Eve" is "increase greatly your anxious toil." What is the impact of this increased anxious toil? How and why do women have the propensity toward anxiety? How does anxiety manifest itself?

DEFAULT BUTTON SET ON ANXIETY

When I get anxious, "But" and "What if" repeat themselves in my head like a broken record. One day during a particularly anxious moment for me, my husband very kindly turned to me and said, "Jackie, I think you have a default button that is set on *anxiety*." I laughed out loud, but then I began to ponder the powerful truth Ken had so casually stated. The remark may seem harsh to you, but it struck me as illuminating: Anxiety is something I have struggled with since I was a little girl. When I think something may go wrong, rather than "default to faith and trust in Papa God," I default to anxiety and try to figure out what I can do about a potential upset of my great plans and blueprints.

When I was a little girl, my sisters and I had to sleep in the attic of my grandmother's house. It wasn't scary during the day, but the nights were often challenging. My little bed had a steel frame and often my parents would have to come and wake me up and tell me that I was shaking so hard in my sleep that the bed frame was making a racket! They would tuck the blankets in really tight to try and curb my shaking. So, from early childhood I can remember the feeling of body-wracking anxiety and fear! What could I possibly have been so anxious about in elementary school? Even at a young age I felt a lot of pressure to get good grades and make my parents proud. Between that perfectionism and family dynamics and anxiety about my parents fighting so often, it's no wonder I would quake in the night.

As I have pondered my anxiety propensity, I came across a perfect verse with which to begin to adjust my default anxiety button: "Be still and know that I am God" (Ps. 46:10). Looking more closely at the two words, "Be still," I discovered that in the Latin translation of the Old Testament, "be still" means "to vacate." Wow—God is inviting me to learn, step by step, how to *vacate* my position of junior god, to take a vacation from worrying about the outcome of my plans and blueprints as wife, parent, friend, author, and speaker. He invites me to repent of my tendency to become anxious when I am not in control, and this is a profound invitation for me as a woman who has lived for years with her default button set on anxiety. When we take Him up on this invitation to go on vacation from anxiety, God's Word tells us that we can *know* that He is God. To know this truth is to live on a perpetual vacation from pushing my default button. (And I have pushed that button so many times in my life that I have arthritis in my tapping finger!)

JUST ANOTHER DAY OUTSIDE THE GARDEN

I have met hundreds of believers who are like Job's friends, always assuming that suffering is a consequence of one's disobedience. Recently, during several back-to-back trials, I was sharing with a friend about my confidence that these trials were not God's judgments, but rather they were "just another day outside the Garden." As I said that phrase, it captured my heart and has become an encouraging guard on my soul against discouragement. After all, as Job put it: "Mortals, born of woman, are of few days and full of trouble" (Job 14:1).

Notice that the days are *few* but these few days are *full* of trouble. Now personally, I would prefer having a life full of *days* with only few troubles. I looked up the word "trouble" in Hebrew, and I found that it means "violent emotion of anger, fear, tremble, torment, rage and restlessness." Consider the reality that our days are full of these negative conditions; however, they are part of "just another day outside the Garden." There is a certain peace that comes from accepting this fact. As Peter writes, "Dear friends, do not be astonished that a trial by fire is occurring among you, as though something strange were happening to you" (1 Peter 4:12, NET).

That list of synonyms for life's challenges should not shock us or derail us. Even though our relationship with God does not immunize us against torment, restlessness or trials, our relationship with God gives each of us privileged access to sufficient grace to sustain us during a day "full of trouble," regardless of the situation.

TREASURES MISSED WHILE WAITING FOR PERFECTION

During a moment of great challenge and chaos, I almost passed on time spent with dear friends. The chaos (our house was half-flooded) seemed like a justifiable excuse not to have friends from Seattle stay in our home. Ken and I decided to welcome our friends anyway, and we learned an invaluable lesson. Too often people miss the treasures that are hidden amidst the trouble and chaos of their lives, while waiting for perfection to be restored or attained. Having guests in our home during the mess and drama of the flood allowed for moments of priceless fellowship that we would have missed waiting for our house to be returned to "perfection"!

Again, as Job put it: "Are God's consolations not enough for you, words spoken gently to you?" (Job. 15:11). If your week has been "full of trouble," don't miss the consolations that God's Word so generously provides.

WHAT CONTROLLING WOMEN FEAR

The more fearful you are, the more controlling you will be. Control, as we've established, is an outgrowth of fear. Does that mean that a woman who has all her ducks in a row is as highly disciplined, perseverant, Type-A, concrete-sequential, and fabulously organized as she appears? Sometimes such driven perfection does not flow from DNA, personality or gifting, but instead from an inordinate fear of people.

One time I witnessed a woman become completely unglued in a small group Bible study because of something "horrible" that had happened at church earlier that day. Someone was supposed to have printed out a list of names that this woman would give to the pastor in the meeting. Well, the assistant forgot the list. When this woman arrived at the staff meeting and was informed that her assistant didn't have the list done, she went ballistic.

So, we're in Bible study and I'm staring at this woman who was even rather hysterical sharing the story. Perhaps not so quietly, I murmured, "Did your first born die? What in the world are you screaming at?"

She exclaimed, "But the pastor needed that list."

"Okay," I responded (probably not really trying to bite my sarcastic tongue), "But did the world come to an end when he didn't get it?"

"No! But you don't understand! I know he doesn't respect me anymore."

At this point I had to dive right in: "Let me tell you something! If your getting that list done is the basis of his respect, then you both have problems." I went on to remind her about the fundamental nature of what she was looking for—love. We don't love based on performance. Jesus doesn't love us that way. While we were yet sinners, He died for us; He loves us. We're called to love each other unconditionally, not proportionally based on performance. God's love is not an If/Then proposition. That mentality holds women hostage. The more panicked people are when things don't go right, the more insecurity is on display. That poor woman's world was shaking with the fear of not being "respected" and cared for by her pastor. One or both of them was being held hostage to a lie. However, I find that when I am afraid, I turn to anything I have control over and proceed to exert control compulsively. For example, I will:

- get my house in perfect order, even the fridge.

- make a to-do list for every day of the week, lining up appointments by neighborhood proximity.

- put my closets in perfect order, sorted by color.

When I do this, I am essentially telling God, "I don't need your help, I can take care of things all by myself." Sounds like a two-year-old to me. Just as Eve did not turn to God for help in answering the serpent's questions when she was in the Garden, so I forget to go first to God and ask Him to take away my fear and to comfort me.

As women, we too often default toward fear when things are going wrong. The more anxious I get, the more I need to figure out how to control this thing. How am I going to fix this? How am I going to work this out? What do the others think? As I have learned to surrender my Junior God Badge, I now have a different reply when I am asked by others, "What is your plan?" I've found that it is actually very unnerving to people when my reply is, "I'm not going to do anything." My friends are incredulous, so I repeat the fact that there is nothing I can do without trespassing into God's territory.

Often, my friends persist, "Come on! You've always got a creative solution. What do you think should be done?"

My final reply, "I'm doing *nothing!* Look at me. No Thing!"

If the more anxious a woman becomes, the more she wants to control, the converse is also true: The more secure a woman is, the less likely she will need to be in control. Isn't that awesome? We will either be controlled by the Holy Spirit or we will be putting on several Junior God Badges with renewed commitment in order to somehow, some way control this chaotic situation. Here are the four very common sources of fear for the Junior God Badge owner.

FOUR THINGS COMMONLY FEARED BY CONTROLLING WOMEN

1. The Fear of the Hypothetical "What If"

2. The Fear of Intimacy (intimacy = "into me see")

3. The Fear of Disappointing People: People-Pleasing Bondage

4. The Fear of Failure: Making a Wrong Choice (failure being fatal for her self-esteem)

These fears are all too common among us. But what does Scripture say about fear?—"There is no fear in love. But perfect love drives out fear, because fear has to do with punishment. The one who fears is not made perfect in love" (1 John 4:18). Let's examine the fears one by one and then see if we can apply God's truth to each one of them.

Fear of the Hypothetical "What If": No Grace for Hypothetical Situations

The controlling woman loses sleep at the first thought of things not going according to her elaborate blueprints. Sweat breaks out on her upper lip when it is even implied that one of her ducks have been knocked out of their perfect row! A controlling woman doesn't lose sleep because she did not actually finish her work; she has insomnia because of the tormenting "what ifs" running through her head. When I am in a "what if" mindset, I have moved into the realm of the hypothetical, and God's grace is not available for such delusional anxiety. I learned the principle of *no grace for the hypothetical* from a deeply godly man whom I dubbed, "my personal prophet." For a couple of decades, this precious brother-in-Jesus, Al Brown, has shared nuggets of profound, life-impacting truths with me whenever we happen to run into each other. I always welcome his input, though sometimes my family does not. One time he caught our whole family together and said, "You're in a storm. You're in a ship without a rudder or a sail." And it was true! We were in such a storm, and no one knew about it except our family. We were all staring in shock when he finished his statement with, "But Jesus is in your boat, too." We all walked to the car in silence, pondering his comment. I saw this brother again after that warning, and he said he had something else to share with me. Being a courageous man, he spoke it out: "Jackie, you constantly have fear of things that might happen. Your compulsion to control is a sign of that fear." I immediately admitted to him that I have lived my whole life with fears such as, "What happens if my kids get sexually abused? What if someone attacks my daughter because she's petite? What if somebody hurts her or rapes her?" Removing my Junior God Badge allowed me to see the danger of being an overbearing mom, a fearful helicopter parent who is so controlling that she actually harms her children through her control. It's as if I was so afraid of my children being harmed that I didn't even see how sharp the blades were on my hovering helicopter over their lives!

Now, why are "what if" fears so crippling? Al told me: There is *no grace for a hypothetical situation*. Grace is available only for reality. Grace is not available for the things that might happen. My delusional fears block God's grace for what will happen, because my fears are not grounded in reality but fantasy. "There they were overwhelmed with dread, when there was nothing to dread" (Ps. 53:5). God's grace is available when we come boldly to the throne of grace in a time of need (see Hebrews 4:16). God's grace is available for *time of need* only, not for the tormented *hypothetical time of need*. God's grace is available and sufficient for today. Right now. The moment I step ahead into the future, I will be anxious, because I am trying to borrow grace from tomorrow. When the torment of "what if" begins in my head, God's grace doesn't go there. God's grace is for *what is* not for *what if*. "So don't worry about tomorrow, for tomorrow will bring its own worries. Today's trouble is enough for today" (Matt. 6:34, NLT).

Now, when I am anxious, I immediately examine my heart for the lurking fantasy of the hypothetical, and I repent and stay in the moment—where grace is. I no longer make excuses when my friends say, "Jackie, don't worry about it." I could always think of good reasons to be panicked. Some people default toward peace; I default toward anxiety, which is sin. "Whatever is not done in faith is sin" (see Romans 14:23). Consider the ridiculousness of thinking, "I am fretting and worrying by faith." Ha! You can justify having sanctified worry?

A wise brother in Christ, George MacDonald, wrote in the late nineteenth century a challenge to those who feel their worry and anxiety is sanctified and justified:

> It has been well said that no man ever sank under
> the burden of the day. It is when tomorrow's

burden is added to the burden of today that the weight is more than a man can bear. Never load yourselves so, my friends. If you find yourselves so loaded, at least remember this: it is your own doing, not God's. He begs you to leave the future to Him and mind the present.

We need to add to our ministry of encouragement of one another this reminder to stay in the present and not trespass into tomorrow's troubles. I rarely hear people say, "Have you admitted or confessed that anxiety to God yet?" I wonder how often we blame God for the burdens we are carrying when we have borrowed burdens from tomorrow where grace is not available. As I was just typing that sentence the Lord brought to my mind something I have borrowed from the future! I needed to pause and ask God's forgiveness for such "faith-less" behavior. We understand the need to turn from the sinful ways of alcohol, drug, and sex abuse, but we almost never confess our sin of borrowing anxiety from tomorrow.

In one of her Bible studies, Beth Moore wrote:

Fear of trials sometimes depletes more energy than facing trials! Help comes to us in times of trouble not before, when we're letting fear and dread overcome us. Once we accept the inevitability of hardship, we can redirect our focus from fear of trials to faithfulness. In the face of tribulations, we often sense a heavenly strength filling our souls right on time.[7]

For many years I have had this fear of getting cancer. Every time something had to be tested in my body, I would break a sweat and fearfully imagine my doctor telling me that I had cancer. When my precious husband got kidney cancer, I was absolutely stunned. He even joked about my being disappointed because it was him and not me; he had witnessed years of my cancer anxiety. Then a sobering day came for me, a cancer expert remarked to a dear friend of mine that the majority of female patients he is treating for cancer are driven, Type A, controlling women! All my worry about getting cancer was the exact kind of mind-set that could create the cancer! The wisest man who ever lived captured this truth thousands of years ago: "A peaceful heart leads to a healthy body; jealousy is like cancer in the bones" (Prov. 14:30, NLT).

A peaceful heart is *never* present in the tormented "what if" woman. My anxiety makes my heart sick and, as someone has said, "Anxiety is the common cold of mental illness."

Fear of Intimacy ("Into me see"): Polished Pretenders

Fear #2 is the *fear of intimacy*, which I like to think of as "Into me see." It's the fear of being vulnerable. Most of us are afraid of people seeing us as we really are. Yet, did you know that most of the New Testament was written by someone who described himself as "chief among sinners?" The Apostle Paul learned so many of the things that he wrote to comfort us out of his struggles with sin. You and I don't have to be chief among sinners; we can let Paul make that claim. But we can learn to be comfortable with our flawed nature, instead of trying to cover it up.

In my book *A Man Worth Waiting For*, one of the chapters described the principle, "faithful though flawed." I've been faithful to Jesus for forty-eight years, but I am still a flawed human. The key is not achieving flawlessness, it's being faithful although flawed.

Some women are scared that someone will find out they're not perfect (and neither are their children or their husbands or their families of origin). But the secret is out: *not one of us is perfect.* And furthermore, *we already know it about each other!* There has been only one perfect person, the Lord Jesus Christ—the spotless Lamb of God. The rest of us are simply flawed "dust."

More than three hundred years ago a woman named Madame Jeanne Guyon was imprisoned in the Bastille in France, because she wrote about Jesus so intimately that some of the local church fathers didn't like the way she expressed her intimacy with Jesus. She was defined as "a woman who loved Christ too much." Living for years in isolation in a cold damp cell only made her grow in her love for Christ rather than making her bitter. After leaving prison she began writing again out of her realistic view of human life: "With a true spirit of His humility, you will not be surprised at your faults, your failures, or even your own basic nature. You and I are very weak, and at our best we are very weak."

How often do you find yourself amazed when you make a poor or unwise choice? Are you shocked when another Christian fails? Madam Guyon's quote is a reminder that we should be shocked only by the *fact that we are shocked* when a person fails. Why are you surprised? All humans, without exception, even on their best day, are simply dust: "As a father has compassion on his children, so the Lord has compassion on those who fear Him; for He knows how we are formed, He remembers that we are dust" (Ps. 103:13-14).

If you have a day of apparent success, it means Jesus is reigning on the throne of your heart. But during your stressed-out, discontented moments, "simply dust" is reigning on the throne of your heart (see Psalm 51:6).

One day in Vicki Courtney's book, *Move On*, I read a quote that so grabbed my heart that I had to write to Vicki about it. Here are her words: "Many of our churches have ceased to be hospitals for messed-up people and opted instead to become showrooms for polished pretenders."

Do you attend such a church? Do you fellowship with people who are unwilling to risk intimacy lest you find out that they also are a hot mess, like you? Almost immediately I got an email reply from Vicki, and she said I could share her words in this book:

> Jackie, your kind words mean so much. What you don't know is that you were a major inspiration for me writing that book. Honestly, you were one of the first believers I met who refused to play "the pretender game." It was so refreshing and I knew the moment I met you that I wanted to be like you—raw honesty steeped in grace.

Thank *you*, sister, for the amazing influence you
have been in my life.

It truly is amazing that being real and not pretend-
ing could be such an inspiration. All my life people have
commented about my being so candid and "real." At first
I would respond with the remark, "I am a follower of the
Truth—candidness and being real seems inevitable!" Then
I realized how many people are so afraid of being real, and
I marveled anew at the amazing grace Jesus has lavished on
me for the past forty-eight years. "How great is the love the
Father has lavished on us, that we should be called chil-
dren of God! And that is what we are!" (1 John 3:1).

The Fear of Disappointing People: People-Pleasing Bondage

The fear of intimacy and vulnerability actually feeds
this next fear—the bondage of "people-pleasing." People
pleasing looks nice and accommodating on the surface,
but it amounts to saying and doing whatever you think
will keep others happy—because you are afraid of displeas-
ing them. The underlying motive is to protect yourself.
It's a subtle way of control at times, because it can *look*
like just being nice or accommodating. The only way to
identify people-pleasing is to ask the Holy Spirit to reveal
your motives.

One woman cheerfully packs up her four young children every Sunday afternoon to go to her mother-in-law's
for dinner. Another young mom organizes her brood to go
to Grandma's every Sunday, quietly resenting the upheaval

and the assumptions. She "suffers in silence," however, because she is sure that people will be furious with her if she asks to alter the plans. She tries to protect herself from their bad opinion or bad mood by "doing the right thing"—even if "the right thing" is actually saturated with deception.

In one's desperate attempt to please people incessantly, there is no room or tolerance for being flawed. What is so desperately sad about this fear of disappointing people, is that it's fueled daily by insecurity. Women work very hard to cover up the blemishes of their insecurity, and the make-up they so often use is people-pleasing. The controlling woman believes if she can please everyone, she will be loved and accepted by everyone. Jesus condemned people-pleasing, and Paul warns us about vain pursuit:

> *Everything they do is done for people to see.* (Matt. 23:5)

> *Am I now trying to win the approval of human beings, or of God? Or am I trying to please people? If I were still trying to please people, I would not be a servant of Christ.* (Gal. 1:10)

Paul is saying that when I am a people-pleaser I am not a servant of Christ. People-pleasers are slaves to the opinions and preferences of others. When I am worried about pleasing people, I have ceased to be concerned about God's agenda for me, and I cannot please Him. I please Him when I co-labor with God as a servant in His Kingdom (see 1 Corinthians 3:6-9).

"Fearing people is a dangerous trap, but trusting the Lord means safety" (Prov. 29:25, NLT). Fearing people escorts me to a jail cell—cramped, damp and depressing. Trusting in the Lord escorts me to a wide open field where I can run free in the sunshine—beyond the grip of suffocating people-pleasing.

But I must warn you, when you stop pleasing people, they are no longer pleased with you.

As I have learned to surrender my Junior God Badge, I have learned how to let Him take care of the people who are aggravated because I am not pleasing them today. Somebody might say to me, "Oh Jackie, if you don't come, so-and-so is going to be so mad at you." And I reply, "Well, before the sun sets, she will have to confess to God her anger toward me for not coming." On a regular basis, a "recovering people-pleaser" will have several people disappointed with her, and she needs to pray that they will release their disappointment and anger before the end of the day (see Ephesians 4:26-27).

The controlling woman doesn't realize that her passionate pursuit of pleasing everyone will make her vulnerable to what I call *Christian blackmail*. When I was a brand-new Christian, I was completely controlled by every Christian I met. One said to me, "Wow, you shouldn't wear that color of nail polish," so I took the nail polish off.

I am a totally wild woman for Jesus and I have often been criticized for being too loud and too enthusiastic. I used to feel condemned for not manifesting a "gentle and quiet spirit" a la Peter's description of a godly woman (see

1 Peter 3:3-4). Then I looked it up and realized that a meek (gentle) and quiet spirit refers to *not being anxious,* not to having a quiet personality or voice. In fact, a controlling woman may conceal her anxious spirit with a controlled, soft voice.

The Fear of Making Wrong Choices

I have met many women who cannot relate to the previous three sources of fear. That kind of woman does not care what others think about her. She is candid and outgoing and is not afraid of being vulnerable and she doesn't fear the hypothetical, because she moves so fast toward the future that she doesn't even stop and consider the probability of things not going as her controlling self has planned. But I have discovered a fourth source of fear that affects even the apparently invincible ones—the *fear of making the wrong choice.* An otherwise competent woman can be incapacitated by her fear of making the wrong choice.

Some people are so afraid of making a wrong choice, they can't even make a right choice. It's called the "paralysis of analysis." (Although when you're so afraid of making the wrong choice, the fact is, *that is* a choice.) This paralysis can occur around some of the simplest choices like what to order on a menu or whether to buy the light blue socks or the dark blue ones. It's not because it's such a difficult decision with grave consequences; the fear is just that the choice is not the best or wisest one. Do you know that expression, "The best is the enemy of the good"?

Well, someone stuck in analysis paralysis flips that around to, "The good is the enemy of the best!"

If our measurement of whether a choice is good or bad is the appraisal of God's Word and if the Word doesn't say anything about whether you should go to Weight Watchers or Jenny Craig—do not waste any more brain cells on this decision. Do what works for you in the context of your life. Don't compare your life with others'.

How do you defuse the paralyzing fear of making the wrong choice? First and foremost, understand how God feels about failure. From what I've seen, we get really confused about that. Here's how He feels about your failures. He expects them. He forgives them. He uses them. God is the great "recycler" of the messes we make, and none of them shock Him! "My dear children, I write this to you so that you will not sin. But if anybody does sin, we have an advocate with the Father—Jesus Christ, the Righteous One" (1 John 2:1). Those of us who belong to Jesus have the greatest defense attorney on eternal retainer for us.

Someone who is terrified of doing something wrong doesn't usually realize how perfectionistic this attitude is. This tormented woman does not know that perfectionism is not really even about being perfect; it's about not being hurt or shamed. It's about self-protection, although in the end, it ends up about being miserable—and making others miserable.

On a long road trip with my husband, I was reading Beth Moore's book, *When Godly People Do Ungodly Things* out loud to him. I had just begun reading a section on

First Samuel 12:20-25, when suddenly my usually-soft-spoken husband yelled, "Stop!" I reread the paragraph. A verse jumped out at me, and I realized what God had just shown Ken through Samuel's statement to the people of Israel:

> *"Do not be afraid,"* Samuel replied. *"You have done all this evil; yet* **do not turn away from the Lord,** *but* **serve the Lord with all your heart.** *Do not turn away after useless idols"* (1 Sam. 12:20-21, emphasis added).

My husband is a very black and white person who struggles when godly people do ungodly things. But in that moment, God gave Ken an epiphany, showing him clearly how King David, who failed terribly, was still called "a man after God's own heart." And after David's great failure, he did not turn away from the Lord. The key is not to think you can avoid failure, but rather *not to turn away from the Lord in your failure.* In the context of God's grace, failure is never fatal.

For too many Christians, however, failure *is* fatal. Too often when a Christian fails, instead of repenting (like David in Psalm 51) and turning back to Jesus and the encouragement of spiritual siblings (as in Hebrews 3:13), the one who has failed goes deeper into sin and shame. I have seen so many in Christian ministry fail and end up turning away from the Lord to "useless idols." The body of Christ is supposed to be a safe place in which flawed people can fail without being slandered on social media or shunned, but rather be assured of prayers for healing (see James 5:16).

The following chapters will reveal the different roles a fearful, controlling woman takes on each day as she attempts to hang on to her Junior God Badge, usurping various aspects of God's job description. While she justifies her sanctified worrying as "just being responsible," in fact she is desperately trying to reign over her little portion of the universe as a wannabe deity. She wants to be like Him, so just call her:

- *Wannabe Omnipresent*

- *Wannabe Omnipotent*

- *Wannabe Omniscient*

- *Wannabe Jehovah-Shalom*

- *Wannabe Sovereign*

I don't want to be a wannabe deity, do you? Take a deep breath and consider the freedom that will come once you realize the areas in your life where you are too focused on being a wannabe deity. When you finish the next five chapters, you may actually be ready to have a Surrender Your Junior God Badge ceremony!

DISCUSSION QUESTIONS

1. Do you, like the author, have a default button set on anxiety? Have you tried to do anything about it? Have your efforts been successful? (See Philippians 4:6-7.)

2. Which of the following statements describe your ultimate fear:
    *   Fear of being vulnerable (See Psalm 51:6.)
    *   Fear of disappointing people (See Matthew 23:5; John 12:43.)
    *   Fear of making wrong choices (See 1 Samuel 12:20-25.)

3. Discuss this statement: "A sure formula for failure: try to please everyone." (See Galatians 1:10; 1 Samuel 16:7.)

4. Discuss this principle: "There is no grace for hypothetical situations." (See Psalm 53:5; Matthew 6:34.) Read 1 John 4:18 and discuss the "what if?" torment.

5. Have you ever experienced Christian blackmail? Share your vulnerable moment so others can grow and be free. (See Matthew 10:16.)

6. How often do you experience a *paralysis of analysis* when making decisions impacting

your life and others? How do you see yourself getting more confidently decisive? (See Proverbs 3:5-6; Proverbs 16:3.)

CHAPTER 3

WANNABE OMNIPRESENT

While sitting in an audience one day years ago, waiting to walk to the platform to teach this material, the MC announced that some of the ladies created a "cheer" for my message, "Surrender Your Junior God Badge." Four enthusiastic women ran to the platform with arms lifted, shaking pompoms, and led out this cheer: *Jesus! Jesus! He's our Man, if He's too busy, MOM can!*

Of course the audience burst into laughter, and I joined right in. When the laughter died down, I walked to the podium and began to talk about the illusion of control—and even omnipresence—in the life of the Junior God Badge owner.

The omnipresent woman strives to live the definition of omnipresent—to be in all places at all times. What is breathtaking about this woman, whether she is, young, old, matronly, spry, whatever—she is always zooming, zooming, zooming, because she has to be everything to everybody. She has got to be at every one of her children's practices, even though there are three kids and three different sports. But watch her! She's at every one of them—even if for only a few minutes to drop off their energy drinks. She's got to be at every one of her children's games—even if she only sees five minutes of every game. Her husband's running in, she's running out…there's a revolving door installed at that house! Being a wannabe omnipresent woman is a very demanding lifestyle. Daily she strives to pattern herself after her omnipresent God. Her favorite verse is this: "Where can I go from your Spirit? Where can I flee from your presence?" (Ps. 139:7)

As my children became older, sadly, this became the groan of their heart in relation to their wannabe omnipresent mom—where can we flee from her presence? Our son would be on the soccer field, and one of the kids would nudge him and say, "Um, I just heard your mom! She's here…she's always here, Ben." They couldn't flee from me. I was the hovering "helicopter mom" who felt *compelled* to be ever-present. Years later when our son was an adult, he mentioned that he felt sorry for me because I had lived in so much fear of missing an event in his life. He said, "Mom, if you had missed a game I would not have died. You have always been there for Jessi and me, but you just didn't know how over-the-top you were." What he was perceiving, even as a boy, was my anxiety, my fear of disappointing my children. That unbridled enthusiasm for my kids was fueled by that old fear of letting someone down. What would happen to *me* if I let someone down? Ironically, when we over-parent, we do as much damage as the under-parenting that a lot of us, including me, got. I became a helicopter parent in reaction to that childhood neglect.

The wannabe omnipresent woman feels overly committed to being *everything* to her family. She is so consumed with every need of every person in her family, living breathlessly to meet those needs, that her family members might as well start lighting candles in worship of the wannabe deity in their midst. The omnipresent, controlling mom smiles when she reads Psalm 139:7 (see above), because it reminds her of…herself! "Where can I go from *her* spirit, where can I go from *her* presence?"

I will always want to be there for my kids. I am absolutely passionate about it. But a good mom does not have to be a Junior Messiah. I was the mom driving in the middle of the night so that my kids and their friends could toilet paper the youth pastor's house! We had so much fun, but I never even considered the possibility of saying "No" to this middle-of-the-night adventure. (In fact, it is one of my kids' favorite memories. And as I type this, I realize that my driving the kids that night was the best place for me…but my doing a thousand other things prior to and following that 1:00 A.M. adventure—that was the problem!)

A young pastor's wife named Rebecca Croft Sellers writes:

The desire for control creeps up in the good and bad. Like a weed that is not yanked up with its roots, in my own strength, control will surface somewhere new—same heart struggle with a different look. Today, I may recognize that my husband is making an important family decision for us. Today, I may recognize that I can't control if my child throws up Fruit Loops after an unneeded snack in class. But tomorrow, I could be a sinful perfectionist by making sure that the pigs in a blanket are rolled and placed evenly. Tomorrow, I may be frustrated to tears, because the party has to be moved indoors but I only bought a rectangular tablecloth for a picnic bench.

This curse is mine, because I am a sinner. However, the power of the cross exchanges its filth for His beauty. When I repent by seeking His forgiveness and turning away, He trades my pride for His humility. He trades my fear of people for awe of Himself and His glory. My obedience is a by-product of His love. Obedience to Him puts my control issues to death. A wise Christ-like friend once told me "Blessed are the flexible, for they are not easily bent out of shape."

SHE FEEDS THE IMPULSE OF IDOLATRY

The omnipresent wannabe trains her family so well that they learn to depend on mom more than God. And it's not just for one's immediate family, the extended family—parents, siblings, in-laws, et cetera—get trained, too. When my sister was dying from an overdose of Quaaludes, I was speaking at a youth conference. Unbeknownst to me, my family of origin was leaving frantic messages on my answering machine, shouting "Call us!! Call us!!" (I didn't get the messages until after she had died.) Of course they were in a panic and wanted to alert me, but here's where the distortion comes in: When my youngest brother finally had a chance to speak to me, he said, "If you had been here, I know she wouldn't have died." Can you hear the echo of someone else's words? That's what Martha said to Jesus about Lazarus! My own savior behavior had convinced them that I actually could have saved our sister from this tragedy.

Letting our family depend on us for their spiritual needs makes us not only the "God Person" but ultimately an idol. We move with such discipline and effectiveness that people depend on us, rather than God. This grooms people to worship the Junior God Badge wearer rather than the only One who can rescue us from ourselves. Ultimately it leaves no room for God. God wants to wean people from depending on the one who wears the Junior God Badge. But here's the hard truth: This weaning comes through suffering. "We were crushed and overwhelmed beyond our ability to endure, and we thought we would never live through it. In fact, we expected to die. But as a result, we stopped relying on ourselves and learned to rely only on God, who raises the dead" (2 Cor. 1:8-9, NLT).

When your child goes through a tough time, and you try to erase any evidence that things were hard, your child will never, ever learn to rely on God more that you. There's nothing wrong with being a great mom, wife, aunt, sister, daughter-in-law, or friend. The reality I am here to tell you, however, is that you are a precious person, *but you are a lousy God!*

Now, there is nothing wrong with striving to be like Proverbs 31 woman, but that is *an ideal,* not a goal. The wannabe omnipresent mom is so invested in the lives of her children that she feels emotionally responsible for everything. She blames herself for everything her children struggle with. Once a youth leader said to me, "Mrs. Kendall, God is not going to let you be such a great mom that your children do not need Jesus." I knew the young man was right, but I was not yet willing to take God's crown off my head. Later, I heard Tony Campolo say, "Parents of good kids take too much credit, and parents of bad kids take too much blame." Let that one sink in! *Selah.*

Consider these wise words from a woman named Mary Lou White:

> Women, and more specifically, moms are often looked to as the cook, cleaning lady, organizer, secretary, lost and found superintendent, pet feeder/walker, laundress, or, let's just say, controller of almost all family/house goings-on. I remember when growing up, it was, "I don't know, ask Mom." She was supposed to know everything. The women become in control by default.

The same could be applied to an office situation, where a woman administrative assistant has to keep track of virtually all information and schedules for a person or a team. Her job description requires her to be "in charge."

These responsibilities of being in control can easily seep into her spiritual life, and she could quite proudly pin on the Junior God Badge, probably without even knowing it was happening. Being "in charge" is so much a part of her life, it becomes a natural part of her thinking/acting (mental) process. After so much seeping, that mentality becomes a flood of actions that cover the very foundation of faith she should be walking on. Instead, she's swimming in an ocean of control. She needs to "beach," get her footing and walk quietly with dependence on God, not herself.

DON'T TAKE SCORE AT HALF TIME— THE GAME IS NOT OVER YET

If you've got a child who's struggling, I want to encourage you with this particular passage of Scripture. During such a time in the life of one of our children, I was so hysterical that I could not sleep. I tossed and turned and finally got out of bed. I went to the den, and as I clicked on the desk light, God brought this thought to my mind, "Read Isaiah 5." I only needed to read four verses before the Lord opened my eyes and lifted my soul from hysterics to peace. Here is what I read:

*I will sing for the One I love a song about His vineyard: My loved one had a vineyard on a fertile hillside. He dug it up and cleared it of stones and planted it with the choicest vines. He built a watchtower in it and cut out a winepress as well. Then he looked for a crop of good grapes, but it yielded only bad fruit.... **What more could have been done for my vineyard than I have done for it?** When I looked for good grapes, why did it yield only bad* (Isa. 5:1-4, emphasis added)?

That line jumped off the page: *What more could have been done for my vineyard than I have done for it?* God did everything possible to make His people Israel a fruitful vine, and when He looked, He got sour grapes. I looked up toward heaven and I thought about how Ken and I had prayed and read the Bible to our children every day. We even fasted for our children that they would grow into passionate lovers of Jesus. Ken and I have lived with intentional focus on Jesus and the work He has assigned to those who follow him (see Ephesians 2:10). *What more could Ken and I have done?*

I asked this question out loud to God, and these thoughts poured into to my heart and mind: "Are you wanting to score higher than I? Are you going to raise better kids than my own people? I had Adam and Eve in a perfect relationship, in a perfect garden, in a perfect marriage, and they sinned against me. Are you expecting to score higher than that?" Although those thoughts may seem absolutely foreign and maybe even offensive to you, as I pondered the reality of all that God has done for His people—whether Israel or His Church—I could see thousands of examples of sour fruit growing on the vines where good grapes should have been.

So as my 86-year-old mentor says, "Don't take score at half-time, the game is not over yet." For all of your "not yet" kids, remember Philippians 1:6, which reads, "And I am certain that God, who began the good work within you, will continue his work until it is finally finished on the day when Christ Jesus returns" (NLT). God alone changes people, husbands, children, parents, and friends. The human heart can be very rough and rocky soil. We parents can't work that soil. Only God can plow up that hard earth and send soil softening rains so the seed of God's Word can finally penetrate the heart and bring forth yummy luscious grapes.

DO THEY LOVE YOU FOR YOUR "YES"?

Another common characteristic of the wannabe omnipresent woman is her inability to say the word *No*. Whether it is a whining child or a moaning adult trying to guilt us into a *yes*, the struggle to say *No* is absolutely universal. Whether married or single, the struggle is absolutely universal. We don't want to be labeled mean or uncaring or unloving, so we let ourselves be easily manipulated by others! I know two moms who are well into their 80s, who have suffered much. Their suffering has come from their inability to say *no* to their demanding adult children. Crisis after crisis can be traced back to their heart-wrenching inability to say the "cuss word" *No* to a grown child.

I was attending a conference in Los Angeles in the early 90s when I heard Dr. John Townsend say, "When people love you for your *yes* that is not love. True love will continue even when I have to say *no*." I was so knocked back by that comment that I don't know if I heard another thing he said. I kept thinking, "No wonder my family and relatives love me—because they can always coerce me into a *yes* when deep in my heart I am screaming *no!*"

Shortly after, I was at a wedding reception, and a wonderful Christian counselor was seated at my table. Several of us were talking about our breathless pace and the struggle to say *No* to family and friends. After listening to all of us for a while, this counselor said something profound: "Girls, when we say *Yes* when in our heart we want to say *No*, the internal *No* will grow into resentment, and that is sin!" I was blown away and I began to realize that it gives God glory when I tell the truth and say *no,* even when people are pushing for my *yes.* "Then Joshua said to Achan, 'My son, give glory to the Lord, the God of Israel, by telling the truth" (Josh. 7:19, NLT).

Does the thought of saying *no* send chills down your spine? Does the prospect of someone only loving you for your *yes* make you sick to your stomach? Consider the amount of fear that prevents us from giving the true reply of our heart. Too many of our replies are simply a reflection of the tyranny of fear!

The Lord gave me the greatest way to say *no*. This little line has been a gift to my very handicapped soul: "Oh, how I would love to say *yes*, but I am going to have to say *no*. Thank you for thinking of me." Now I'm actually having a little fun saying *no*. Also, I have learned that I need to be gracious when others tell me "No." I certainly don't want to be guilty of loving people only for their *yes*.

"There is no fear in love. But perfect love drives out fear, because fear has to do with punishment. The one who fears is not made perfect in love" (1 John 4:18).

Notice the connection between fear and punishment? Many of us have spent too many years being terrorized by family and friends who attack us verbally as not being a "loving Christian," because we said no (for example—saying no to bailing a family member out of jail again). Sometimes these verbal attacks have so hurt me that I end up changing my *No* to *Yes*. Not one second after I have said yes, I remember, *"They love you only for your yes!"*

I have met thousands of women who are taken captive daily by the demands of others. These dear women never have even a moment to ponder whether or not the LORD would have her do one thing or another. When you combine a woman's fear with her need to control, there is little time to reflect before responding. Only reflective pauses will allow you and me to frisk our thoughts and hesitations, examining whether fear produced or love produced our response. Too often I am swept up in another person's crisis that is a result of poor planning, and it becomes my emergency! All of us wannabe omnipresents should get one of those plaques that says, "Your crisis is not my emergency!"

For too many years I have been a *Yes* person. I never wanted anyone to think I wasn't a good Christian, so I rarely said *No* to anyone in need. This fear was enhanced by my dysfunctional upbringing that produced a person who was terrified of ever letting anyone down and having anyone disappointed with me. I said yes to everything my pastor ever asked me to do and yes to every Christian in need, because I didn't want anyone to not love me. I didn't realize that saying *yes* was so tied up with being loved. I had no idea. Such fear is not love.

Our wise *No* will allow us to raise children who don't think the world revolves around them. It is easy for the parents' world to revolve around their children, but we need to be careful to teach them that the world does not revolve around them. People often complain about how "me-centric" our culture is, but the woman who cannot say no to her children has helped populate this very culture. Dr. Larry Crabb in the early 90s referred to the me-centric life style as a "demanding spirit." He warned that children are not only harmed by the lack of boundary on their demanding spirit, but that marriages are harmed when a spouse has a demanding spirit. Indeed, adults can also make everyone miserable if they don't get their way, because they're not getting the *yes* they always expect from those around them.

After my father's funeral, I gathered the courage to ask his oldest sister, my aunt, a critical question about him. (My father was the youngest of eleven children.) When I finally had a private moment with Rita, I asked her, "Was my father abused as a child?" His sister replied immediately with the following: "Oh yes, Johnny was abused all right.

He was allowed to grow up thinking the world revolved around him, and that is the greatest abuse of a child." Talk about motivation to learn how to do better with my own children, learning to say no to the things that feed the demanding spirit that assumes the whole world exists to serve "me"!

On the *Today Show* a few years ago, Kathy Lee Gifford was being interviewed by Matt Lauer in relation to a new children's book. During the interview, he made a comment about her "really great kids." Then he asked her, "Can you think of something specific that you and Frank did with your children that resulted in such great kids?" Kathy responded: "One of the things we were careful to communicate was that the world did not revolve around them. We know many selfish adults who were raised thinking the world revolved around them, and we didn't want to raise that kind of adults!" Kathy stated exactly what my dad's sister shared with me that day of the funeral.

You know what can happen when you say no to your child. The whining and badgering begins. This behavior is totally predictable. Whining is powerful means of manipulating a person to finally surrender to the wishes of the whiner. Even strong Samson was manipulated by a "whining wife" (see Judges 14:16-17). If my mother's *no* is a manifestation of love, my kids' whining and badgering is a manifestation of self-love. When my kids were younger, I didn't know this. I so wanted their love that I was honestly afraid to say *no*, for fear they wouldn't love me. I believe that I have finally learned that *no* is more loving than *yes* when it comes to being manipulated by one's kids, spouse, friends, and relatives.

HASTE WITH A CALM SPIRIT

Since the wannabe omnipresent has so many things to squeeze into every second of every minute of every hour, she only knows one speed—fast. She is described as always being in a hurry. As I worked to take off my Junior God Badge and stop trying to be omnipresent, I wrote the following short devotion:

> John Wesley wrote, "Though I am always in haste, I am never in a hurry, because I never undertake more work than I can go through with calmness of spirit."
>
> I am trying a new thing. When there are many things screaming for my attention, I pause and I evaluate the projects with this question in mind: *What can I do and remain calm in spirit?* Today my desk, dining room table and kitchen counter were covered with paper work that was screaming for attention. Then I got a call from a dear friend whose mother-in-law was just killed in a car accident. I paused and asked myself, *What can I do and remain calm in spirit?* In that short reflective moment, I felt a holy nudge from God. In calmness of spirit I knew I was to drive to my friend's house and weep with those who were weeping. Then I calmly asked if there was anything I could do for them. They needed a ride to

the airport. At 5:32 P.M. my desk, dining room table and counter tops were still piled high with paper work, but dinner was in the crockpot and I could leave to pick up my friends and take them to the airport—and everything had been done with calmness of spirit.

A couple days later, a friend called to ask if I could go somewhere within the hour. I paused and asked myself, *Can I squeeze this into my day and remain calm in spirit?* The answer was clear—Nope! She was disappointed, but the calmness in my spirit was so satisfying that I wasn't thrown into a whirlwind of guilt over saying *no* to my sweet friend. This reflective pause with consideration of *calmness of spirit* has really helped me say *no* without feeling guilty. The Word expresses the value of: "the unfading beauty of a gentle and quiet spirit, which is of great worth in God's sight" (1 Pet. 3:4).

The gentle and quiet spirit of 1 Peter 3:4 does not mean a quiet personality but calmness of spirit. What a blessing to know that I do not have to live breathlessly to be of great worth to God. I can remove my Junior God Badge, because I don't have to live in a breathless hurry, foaming at the mouth like a rabid raccoon, to impact the world for Jesus. *Yahoo!* (Many of my friends have prayed that I would cease living like a foaming rabid believer!)

In order to apply the "John Wesley Principle," one must surrender his or her Junior God Badge and resign from trying to tame an untamable world. Are you ready to retire from being Head Chick in Charge or Head Rooster in Charge? Early retirement from an ill-fitted burden is within our grasp today: "Be still, and know that I am God…." (Ps. 46:10).

BEWARE OF CHRONIC PARTIAL ATTENTION

The omnipresent wannabe deity has her own Radio Shack in her purse: beepers, cell phones, iPads, back-up batteries—all the tools of an omnipresent woman! (Have you noticed that women no longer carry purses? They have traded them in for mini-suitcases.)

What has been happening with the growth of technology is a dangerous CPA. No, I am not referring to your bookkeeper. I am referring to the state of "chronic partial attention." A woman may think that all her technology allows her to soar in her pursuit of being a wannabe omnipresent deity, but ironically, the more technology she uses, the more distracted she becomes, not giving full attention to any one thing. Everyone in her life is receiving the crumbs of chronic partial attention. What is even more frustrating and dangerous is that everyone is impacted by CPA, because everyone has smart phones that allow them to live in a chronic distracted state, so that nothing ever gets full attention—not parents, not teachers, and especially not God.

Here is a major *No* to consider and incorporate in your home: *no* cell phones at the dinner table. Put out an attractive basket on a counter in the kitchen where all phones and iPads can be placed during meal time. Families don't even talk to each other anymore because of this epidemic of CPA.

BE READY FOR INEVITABLE DISAPPOINTMENT

There is so much unnecessary suffering for the Junior God Badge owner because of lists of unrealistic expectations. She learns to master disappointment by being realistic about her expectations.

One day our son Ben shared a quote that had such a profound impact on me that I now try to include it in every book I write. Drum roll:

Expectations are pre-meditated resentment.[8]

After he shared it with me, as I drove around doing errands, I replayed hundreds of situations from my life where I could clearly trace the expectations that preceded the resentment in my heart. Then I remembered a quote characterizing resentment as "drinking poison and hoping the other person dies." If my expectations are inextricably linked to pre-meditated resentment, then I am poisoning myself when I don't immediately commit those expectations to God (see Psalm 62:5). Just as we are encouraged in the Word to take our thoughts captive (see 2 Corinthians 10:5), we can extend that idea to expectations. Now I envision myself carrying a leather lasso so I can take captive any expectation that comes into my heart and mind. Then I can tie that expectation to the cross.

Reflecting on my many expectations—all my pre-meditated resentments—it is no wonder I can be prone to sulking disappointment. I heard Brennan Manning say at a conference, "Expectations are our subtle attempt to control God and manipulate mystery." I must begin with God, asking His forgiveness for my controlling expectations. Then I ask His forgiveness for all the slow-burning resentment in my heart because of so much desire mixed with grief—so many expectations...of myself...of others...of life.

A controlling woman needs to remove her Junior God Badge and then, in a prayerful moment of faith, again present her longings, lists, and desires to God, asking to know His Will. Only by surrendering myself to *His* expectations for my life can I relinquish my own. The Holy Spirit reminds us to give our blueprints and dreams to the Lord for His authorization on a continual basis. He tells us to preface our plans with the expression, "If the Lord wills..." When I focus on my dreams and my plans and my expectations without giving one thought to God's script and God's dream and God's plans, I disregard the highest good for my soul. Again, the psalmist nails it: "But now, Lord, what do I look for? My hope [expectation] is in You" (Ps. 39:7).

WANTING A "10" LIFE IN A "5" WORLD[9]

I have a good friend who was battling with a low-grade depression, an inevitable by-product of being a controlling woman. Trying to be omnipresent or omnipotent is so exhausting that depression is not a surprising result. If you looked at this woman's life, you would say, *How can you possibly be depressed?* This woman has it all, but having it all has not kept her immune from a low-grade fever of depression that runs through her soul.

Recently, she had an epiphany in the counselor's office when she was introduced to the principle of wanting a "10" life in a "5" world. The counselor helped her to see that she wants life to be a 10, but life outside the Garden of Eden is too often a 5 (or less). These unmet expectations were fueling her constant trouble with depression.

When the controlling woman tries to arrange circumstances so that her life is a 10, her high expectations produce resentment and depression when all she encounters is the "5" reality of life outside the Garden. In various ways, we are all like this woman, wanting life to be perfect. We want to be able to plan our day and have things go according to our nice neat plan. We want to work hard to prepare a special event and have everyone do their part to make it a success. We want to go on vacation and build some wonderful relaxing memories, without every member of the family getting food poisoning. We want to be able to sacrifice to provide something wonderful for those we love without having the event or occasion turn out less than satisfying.

Mastering disappointment is only possible when you plan a 10 vacation or a 10 holiday gathering or a 10 event if you are then sure to guard your heart when you get a 5 as the result of all your holy sweat!

I love holidays, and I work very hard to make sure I have the time to prepare all the many things that make a holiday most memorable with loved ones. Yet one thing I tend to forget in my preparations for a specific celebration is to prepare my heart for the reality of potential disappointment and offense. Too often I am outwitted by the same relative who repeats the same offensive behavior during every festive celebration. I can have my house decorated just as I imagined and all the food turn out perfectly, only to forget to remind my heart that life is always more chaotic than predictable. I need to leave room for this much-anticipated event to be a 5, not the 10 I dreamed of. I also need to remind myself that even on a most special holiday such as Christmas I may need to forgive someone I love for doing something that offends me.

Was last Christmas or Thanksgiving a disaster because of a selfish relative? Include emotional care of your own heart in your holiday preparations, in anticipation of the inevitable probability of disappointment. Protect your heart from the fantasy that this time will finally be a 10, because it will not happen.

DISCUSSION QUESTIONS

1. How do you spend much of your day hurrying to be "omnipresent" for those you love? (See Psalm 139:7.)

2. How may you have you trained your family to be totally dependent on you? (See 2 Corinthians 1:8-9.)

3. How is it difficult for you to say *no* to a loved one—family or friend? Who is the hardest person for you to say *no* to? (Husband, child, best friend, employer, etc.)

4. "They only love me for my yes!" Consider the tyranny of fear that prevents you from giving the reply of your heart. How does that comment give you the courage to consider saying no more often? (See Acts 20:24.)

5. "Expectations are pre-meditated resentment." Discuss this quote, along with the theory about expecting a "10" in a "5" world. Do you agree or disagree with this concept? (See Psalm 39:7.)

6. What do you think of the quote: "Don't take score at half time, the game is not over?" (See Philippians 1:6; 1 Thessalonians. 5:24.) Are you quick to give up hope?

CHAPTER 4

WANNABE OMNIPOTENT

She strives to be omnipotent. The controlling woman is a wannabe omnipotent deity, the ultimate example of someone with the messiah complex. Omnipotence refers to being all-powerful, and this wannabe omnipotent woman is filled with bigger-than-life expectations for not only herself but others, too. Like her sister, Wannabe Omnipresent, she runs at a pace like the Energizer Bunny, because she assumes she has unlimited power. She has unrealistic, grandiose expectations of herself; and, in fact, the harder this woman is on herself, the harder those around her will often experience her—encountering her as a whip-wielding Pharaoh! Whether in the workplace or in the home, this omnipotent wannabe is striving daily to be seen as Wonder Woman. What this wannabe omnipotent woman thinks she can accomplish in a day is beyond delusional.

All women face pressure and unrelenting demands on their time, but I believe the Christian woman has even steeper challenges. Followers of Jesus have the heightened sense of responsibility to be the best Christian as well as the best wife and mom and employee. They put pressure on themselves from Scriptures such as this simple statement: "Whatever you do, work at it with all your heart, as working for the Lord, not for human masters" (Col. 3:23).

I have heard so many messages in the church calling for intentional excellence in every area of our lives. I am all for doing my best, but an unspoken message among too many Christian women is that *the best is the only grade*—there is no room for a "B" day in one's life. For the omnipotent wannabe, less than the best is not acceptable, and failure is fatal.

Ultimately, this mentality of excellence is a handicap for the wannabe omnipotent woman. She never gets a break. She is expected to perform and do and serve even when she is running a fever. I am embarrassed to say that during the many years that I was a loyal Junior God Badge owner, I would get on a plane to travel and speak—even when I had walking pneumonia. As an omnipotent Junior I had an over-inflated view not only of my responsibility but also my capacity.

I am not the only one guilty of an over-inflated view of my responsibility. I know hundreds of moms who cook meals for their families when they are deathly ill. That kind of woman feels that no one can take care of her family as well as she can. She drags herself into the kitchen to prepare dinner or into the basement to do seven loads of laundry when *truly* someone else could do it, or it could wait a day, or something in the freezer could just be microwaved.

Does the following situation sound familiar to you? Here is some very personal musing of mine: *Don't you just hate it when you have just arrived home from being away for a few days and you are barely in the door and the gang wants to know "what's for dinner?" I have been out of town shedding blood emotionally and when I arrive home, I need some TLC or a blood transfusion! I have fantasized that my family would jump up and say, "We are taking you out to dinner, Mom, because we know you are exhausted." Or if you have worked all day and you walk through the door and the family is all in front of the TV and they barely greet you but they boldly ask, "What's for dinner?" This used to really yank my chain and light my fuse until the Lord showed me that I created this total mommy-dependent gang. They are the monster of my own creation!*

JARGON OF THE WANNABE OMNIPOTENT WOMAN

The wannabe omnipotent has her own special language for communication. Here are a few of her most often-used daily expressions:

- I can do it, wait a minute.

- I'll get it.

- Let me get off the phone, just give me a minute.

- I'll be there.

- I'll fix it.

- Give me a minute, don't worry, I'll take care of it.

- Here, let me do that.

- I can add that to my schedule.

These lines flow from a woman whose schedule was packed before her alarm went off in the morning. She is attempting to add "just one more thing" to a plate that she'll have to exchange for a platter by lunchtime! Once she's got her day all planned out, then comes the phone call that adds one more activity to an already overloaded schedule. This wannabe omnipotent isn't just en route for carpool, she's en route to a meltdown! She's striving to be what only God can be—*omnipotent*.

Why do you think so many women in America are depressed? Why are so many women using prescription drugs or alcohol to cope with the pace of their lives? Why do you think so many women engage in "mall therapy" to take the edge off their breathless pace of life?

What is so tragic about trying to be omnipotent is that you're involved in too many things that God never even put into your script. I hear from women weekly who are having "meltdowns," and the ones falling apart are usually the wannabe omnipotents. I hate to have to tell these women in their weakest moments that this has happened because of pride. That may seem harsh, but keep it in mind as you read the rest of this chapter. As Obadiah said, "You have been deceived by your own pride" (Ob. 1:3, NLT).

One hyper-focused college student named Carly Stupenski emailed: My room with all my calendars and schedules for the coming semester sprawled out around me. Multiple to-do lists on different receipts, post-its, napkins, you name it. My computer open to my flight schedule and my email to see make sure I wasn't missing anything. I sat there for a good 20 minutes rifling through everything, trying to sort it out, and I got so worked up over all that I have already committed to and what needs to get done so soon. My response should have been to hand control of it all over to the Lord and ask that His kingdom work be done through it all. I should have breathed deep into His control and strength and power, but instead I ran out to CVS to buy a planner to take control of the situation. I went to bed anxious after penciling in everything for the coming year—and then this morning I read your article on control. This struck a chord, and I'm so thankful for the reminders like these that *I can't be superwoman.* Praise Him!

As a young mama who is slowly being weaned from being a total omnipotent wannabe wrote to me:

> I have been thinking about your comments about the strength of pride—you are right. It is pride that says I can do it all without going crazy. It is pride that says I can be everywhere and do everything with my kids and make a six figure salary at the same time. It is pride that posts to

Facebook pretending we are all smiles and my life is this envious wonderland (when it often feels like hell)…. I never really recognized that drive can equal pride; there is a balance that too easily tips the wrong way…. I blame it on my "wiring," but in reality, it is just the same sin nature that we all have.

FAMILY'S FAVORITE IDOL

Although sports and movie stars can be idols for many people, none of these can compete with the idol-worship of the omnipotent mom! How does a woman become her family's idol? This idolatry is slow-growing at first. A woman becomes a mom, and she simply wants to do her best. Now that seems innocent enough, but she's in danger of becoming the family idol. Honestly, families love their moms who build their whole world around their families. Their omnipotent mom will take their pulse daily and determine to raise their level of happiness.

For more years than I can count, I made the happiness of everyone I loved my personal responsibility, and I would gauge my own happiness based on whether those I loved were happy. Consequently, any unhappiness in the camp would cause me deep unhappiness. This happiness setup started long before I was married. When I was only a teen-ager, I would constantly do things to cheer up my mother, whose heart was being broken by the poor choices of her children. I made her happiness my personal responsibility. This pathetic tendency even bled into my Christian walk.

As a young follower of Jesus, I actually felt sorry for *God* because of how poorly some of His kids acted. I think I wanted to be a Jackie Super Christian to try to make up for my rebellious spiritual siblings. Now, you might be thinking, "She's one sick puppy," and you would be right. That is why this topic is so near to my heart. But I have made slow but steady progress in recognizing the lies I have believed and replacing those lies with the pure truth of God's Word.

Now, I have been surrounded by plenty of others who also felt overly responsible for the happiness of their spouses or families. I knew a man whose wife left him. When I asked him why she left, he said, "Because I did not make her happy." This woman held her husband responsible for her happiness. A good friend of mine wrote the following when God started to show her that she's supposed to be a good wife, but she can't be her husband's god: "I cannot fill the hole inside your soul. To ask me to is unfair; you're taking more of me than your share. Look to His Word for the reason; He will answer you in good season. Jesus is your Way, your Truth, your Life; all I'm supposed to be is a wife."

A caring friend gave me a poster that hung for years in my den. It was a perfect reminder: "I can only please one person per day. Today is not your day, and tomorrow is not looking good either."

What is simply amazing to me about one person making an idol of another person is how calm we are about this worship of humans. The Old Testament has hundreds of references expressing God's disdain toward idols; but as controlling women, we never even consider the sin of allowing people to make us an idol.

How does this idolatry develop? *Idolatry happens when I let people trust me to make them happy.* Let's break that statement down. First of all, I don't just mean "happy" like having an enjoyable afternoon. I mean *fundamental happiness*, like filling the "hole inside the soul." Then, notice the verb "let"—I *let* someone get away with this. More likely, I encourage it. As I wrote in chapter 3, we train people to rely on us in all kinds of ways. So, if I know that someone else is trusting *me* to be their happiness savior—and I perpetuate that dynamic—shame on me. Ask the Lord to show you where you are letting people make an idol out of you.

Forty years ago when I was married, I was told as a young Christian wife that God makes a husband holy but the wife is meant to make him happy. I could cry over the days wasted trying to make my husband happy! I know so many burned-out women who have tired so very hard, yet they are not married to happy men. Happiness, is between our husbands and Jesus. If a man is not right with God, a wife can dance on the ceiling and momentarily entertain him, but he will always recede back into the "not a happy camper" mode.

As I've said before, you can be a great wife but you are a lousy God! All those years I was trying to be such a great wife so my husband would be happy, what was I really? A lousy god. I became an idol that my family depended upon to fulfill their happiness. I trained my loved ones that my control would assure their happiness.

Let me reiterate: *Whenever I let someone draw their happiness from me, I have become an idol.* And you may remember the wisdom of Jonah—spoken when he found himself in the stomach of a large fish: "Those who cling to worthless idols turn away from God's love for them" (Jon. 2:8).

When I allow any human to depend on me more than God, I help turn them away from God's love for them. When my husband or my children, or even my friends, rely upon me more than God, I have actually helped them forfeit the grace of God. That makes me so sad, because I only want to turn people toward God, never away from Him. But it simultaneously fires me up and inspires me to remove my Junior God Badge. I am compelled to *get out of the way* so my loved ones can run into the arms of Jesus. No matter how powerful, how awesome, how dependable, how reliable any of us are, how do we think we can compete with God for glory? Why do we allow others to become more intoxicated with us than they are with God?

When somebody else's success determines my peace, I'm just feeding what Jeff VanVonderen calls "an impulse to idolatry." If they're unhappy, I'm unhappy. If they're struggling, I'm struggling. If they're not walking with God, then I'm totally devastated. I've given that person too much control over my life. The Holy Spirit is supposed to be on the throne of my heart. Instead, I'm letting my mother-in-law, my sibling, my mom, my husband, and the grocery store clerk reign over my emotions! The wannabe omnipotent, though she appears strong, is actually incapacitated by this idolatrous relationship with a loved one.

I heard John Townsend confirm this in Los Angeles in the early '90s at a women's luncheon (his book *Boundaries* had just been released). He said, "When a conflict with one significant person can bring us to despair, it is possible that we are putting that person on a throne that only should be occupied by God."

I know too many women who have allowed themselves to be incapacitated by the behavior of a loved one. One woman has lost too much weight and aged ten years because of her grief and despair over the bad choices made by a loved one. This does not have to continue. Have you put a loved one on a throne that only God should occupy, or have you allowed them to put you on such a throne?

WANNABE OMNIPOTENT MOMS ARE THE ORIGINAL DRUG DEALERS

I remember how stunned I was the first time I heard a person say, "Moms are the original drug dealers for their children." What? It means that overbearing moms are so concerned about their child's happiness that they never allow their child to genuinely experience life and its inevitable sadness and disappointment. The wannabe omnipotent mom is always busy using her strength to cheer up her child—with food, movies, constant entertainment. Although these cheer-up techniques eventually don't work, they create a gateway for a child to move into drinking and drugs. This mom is constantly writing prescriptions for the child's next "life owes me a happiness fix," and it is a great disservice to raise a child to think the world revolves around him or her! Not allowing a child to experience the full weight of boredom, rejection, disappointment and discontentment will prove to be a handicap for the child in the years ahead.

When we are constantly anaesthetizing any hurt that our family members feel, this produces an emotional handicap when something traumatic happens in the future. You know the line: Little kids, little problems; big kids, big problems. So what happens when they get bigger? We can't fix those big hurts. And when we can't fix things anymore, they resent us for it, and then they turn to inappropriate means of anesthetizing the hurt.

The book of Proverbs comes through with another zinger: "A servant pampered from childhood will become a rebel" (Prov. 29:21, NLT). If a *servant* is vulnerable to future rebellion through pampering, how much more one's own child?

I have been guilty of extending this treatment to just about anybody who seemed to like the attention. For several years my husband and I taught a spring training Bible study for baseball players and their wives. We got close to several of the ballplayers and had the privilege of mentoring them beyond spring training. The ballplayers would call often to ask either marriage questions or parenting questions, and I was always thrilled to give my wise replies. One year during the Bible study, John Smoltz (Baseball

Hall-of-Famer) said, "I have a new name for Jackie. We should all call her DLJ: Direct Line Jackie." Of course he was referring to my being readily available for him or his wife to call with a question any time of the day. At the time, I smiled and was glad to be there for these growing baseball players and their wives.

Beyond baseball, I have often been called on the phone or approached at church or Bible study with some question about something in the Bible. Once I was called Dial-a-Verse Jackie. Even my daughter, who is a pastor's wife, will text me when she needs to find a particular passage of scripture to address a topic she is speaking on. Although I have always pointed people to Jesus and His Word, it reveals the way this wannabe omnipotent allowed people to turn to me for answers rather than looking things up for themselves. The Bible (or, say, *Strong's Exhaustive Concordance*) is readily available for all.

My Junior God Badge was polished every time someone asked me for advice, and, of course, this fed my over-inflated view what I can do, while pride took a deeper hold of my soul.

STRENGTH THAT BACKFIRES

As I write about over-parenting your children in this book, I figure if I come at this theme from twenty different angles, everyone who reads this can walk away with something helpful. I prayerfully hope that my bad examples will be good for you—I'm a true believer in "good bad examples."

It can be quite a shock when this delusion of omnipotence backfires on you! As a mom I was always checking my kids' moods and checking their pulse for whether they were really growing spiritually or not. Frankly, I acted like a personal assistant to God. I was on call 24/7, and it took me a long time to learn that this over-parenting could actually drive my children away from what I most desired for them. That's what I did with my firstborn. I was driving him away from God, and the more he moved away from God, the more I panicked and scrambled after him—which just drove him further away.

I spent years fantasizing about the day my family would say, "Mom, you are working too hard—please give us some things to do that will lighten your burden!" I told this to a Christian counselor, and she just laughed. (Thankfully, she is a good friend!) She reminded me that fantasizing is an illusion, and that if I need help, my family does not have ESP; I need to *ask* for help.

One Saturday afternoon my family was glued to the TV. As usual, I was running around doing too many things and trying to cook a very nice meal. It dawned on me that no one had offered to help at all—and I was only six feet away from them. So suddenly I started tossing the mail up in the air. After several pieces sailed to the floor, one of my kids noticed. I kept throwing the mail around when the one child tapped the other child. The kids starting pointing at me. Then my husband saw what I was doing and asked, "What in the world are you doing?" Well, now that I had a captive audience, I started to sound off about needing help, but how everyone was glued to the TV. Our oldest, Ben, said, "Mom, you could have just asked for help."

Sometimes, the best thing you could do for your family would be to say, "You know I really want to help you with this, but I just can't." When we act like we're omnipotent, day in and day out, it totally stuns our family when we say we can't do something. Some days I have had this thought, "This group needs to get a new idol, because I can't measure up any more."

NOT A PARAMEDIC

The wannabe omnipotent woman ends up in the role of the emotional paramedic. This tendency can predate adulthood. I can remember walking home from school crying with a sixth-grade friend whose parents were getting divorced. When I became a Christian, I actually thought that being an emotional paramedic was required of anyone who wants to love a hurting world. If the wannabe omnipotent woman is within a hundred feet of anyone in a crisis, she puts on her Junior God Badge and runs to the rescue.

One problem with being an emotional paramedic is that you can spend hundreds of hours in a corner listening to a person in crisis—while missing all the other people around you. Now sometimes such a crisis-corner location is the right spot for a servant of God to be, *if* that's where He has called you. But I have been to too many gatherings where my prideful omnipotence was fueled by serving as the emotional paramedic to one person in crisis. I didn't even think to stop and ask the Holy Spirit to reveal His script to me, compelled as I was to fulfill my omnipotent "destiny." It didn't even occur to me that perhaps my role was to love others who were present.

This woman also ends up being a spiritual paramedic. In 1991, two months following the suicide of my younger sister, a counselor friend encouraged me to go back into counseling. I asked her if she could just counsel me, but she declined and said, "There is an exceptional counselor in this town that I really believe you will benefit from seeing." I remember crying all the way to the appointment, wondering if I was doing the right thing. I admitted to the counselor, Carol Smith, that I didn't think I needed more counseling about my past abuse. She very calmly said, "We are going to look at damage far beyond your abuse."

After only two sessions I learned about the danger of being a spiritual paramedic when she asked me, "Why did you keep going back to your parents' house where your father was still living?"

My immediate reply was, "I am the only Christian in our family, and I need to bring the light of Jesus into their dark lives." Her next question rocked my world. Carol asked me if my dad ever behaved inappropriately toward me when I returned home, and I admitted that he did.

Then came one of the most defining moments in my life. Carol asked me, "Jackie, how many years have you been going over to your parents' house trying to win them to Jesus?"

I answered, "Twenty-three."

"Did your dad ever come to Jesus?"

"No"

"Do you believe that God led you into this sick and unsafe situation—year after year?" The spiritual paramedic in me began to defend my intent, but then Carol asked this question, "Do you think Jesus wanted to lead you into further harm?" Tears began to flow as I thought about all the hurtful times around my dad. The spiritual paramedic mentality had kept me in bondage to that noxious environment.

I tried to defend my role as a spiritual paramedic for my family, but I began to hear my own words, and the tears continued to pour down my face. If I hadn't been clinging to my Junior God Badge so tenaciously, I could have contacted a pastor to reach out to my father. I had a messiah complex that kept telling me, "I've got the light and blood will be on my hands if I don't bring the Gospel to my family members."

As if this weren't earth-shattering enough, she then asked me why I would ever go around my father unaccompanied by my husband. I had a ready answer for that, too. "Oh! My family can be pretty crazy, and I hate for him to be around them."

Carol looked at me with compassion and explained, "Jackie, why do you think God gave you such a godly man? God gave you Ken to protect you." Then I remembered how my family was always on their best behavior around Ken. But because of my Junior God Badge, I was trying to spare him—always assuming that the spiritual paramedic should handle the insanity.

I am no longer my family's spiritual paramedic. I have resigned. I realized that I am not the light. Jesus is the light. He does borrow our bodies to shine in this crazy world, but we need to know when and where and how.

OMNIPOTENT WOMAN SHARING THE MARQUEE WITH GOD

I know this subtitle may sound ridiculous, but it captures the sense of entitlement that an omnipotent wannabe can have. Can you just see it? "Tonight! On Stage with God...It's *Jackie!*" Ha! There she is, center stage, helping God out with the universe, especially with His children, leading people to become more and more dependent on her instead of mentoring them to become independently dependent on Jesus and His Word. Rather than Direct Line Jesus (see Hebrews 4:16), it is Direct Line Jackie.

How do you remove your Junior God Badge and wean people from depending more on you than Jesus? How can you direct someone more to Jesus than to Miss Messiah? One awesome lesson I learned is to ask a person, "What has Jesus told you about this problem?"

The person may respond with, "I don't know, I'm telling *you* about the problem." But it turns her attention in the right direction. This person needs to hear something specific from Jesus and His Word or else she will just keeping telling different people her problem for years and years. God will provide. The God of all Comfort will strengthen whoever will come to Him. (See 2 Corinthians 1:3-4.) He is the only one capable of taking a pit of despair and transforming it into a refreshing well filled with living water.

It is a privilege as a Christian to encourage people, giving them the will to continue when things are hard. But I do them a disservice when I allow them to run to the phone to call me, rather than to the throne to call on Him. Jesus wants me to encourage those in need to sit down with their Bible and expect Jesus to give them a word of comfort. Too often the omnipotent wannabe takes such deep pride in how many people need her that she hesitates to encourage them to take time with Jesus and the Word. Forgive us, God, for our audacity of thinking that we know how best to comfort the weary and broken.

When a woman is suffering, it's great to cook for her, pick up her kids after school, and write her a sweet note, but the thing you've got to pray for her is that she will get a living word, something that really speaks to her. God wants to comfort this struggling person personally, and He will use His Word to administer fresh oxygen to her weary soul. "My soul is weary with sorrow; strengthen me according to your word" (Ps. 119:28). Letting someone depend on you more than God blocks that person's chance of experiencing firsthand God's restorative power.

THE MINISTRY OF ABSENCE

Early in my ministry, an older woman warned me not to allow one woman at a conference to dominate all my time, thereby robbing hundreds of other women a moment of encouragement or simply a holy hug. I have also learned to refer people to professional counselors who can help them, instead of putting on my Junior God Badge. I had to recognize that a wannabe omnipotent is not only attracted to every crisis, she also attracts everyone with a crisis, because she is perceived as someone who can handle the incessant drama and trauma. For years I confused an addiction to drama with ministry. The more regularly I removed my Junior God Badge and pushed people toward God rather than me, the more peace I got. And that peace became something that I actually enjoyed more than the drama.

While taking baby steps toward learning not to be a drama mama, I also learned about what Henri Nouwen calls "the ministry of absence." What does the "ministry of absence" mean? Sometimes I need to *not* be readily available, so that a person will be forced to spend more time with God and less time depending on a human (me). Henri Nouwen got this idea of purposely being absent from people you are ministering to from our Savior himself: Jesus told His disciples that it was necessary for Him to go away so that the Comforter could come: "But very truly I tell you, it is for your good that I am going away. Unless I go away the Advocate will not come to you; but if I go, I will send him to you" (John 16:7).

For the dependent disciples, the prospect of Jesus' absence did not sound very appealing. While they would receive the precious Paraclete and Comforter, Jesus' own Holy Spirit, their dim eyes of faith could not comprehend it yet, not until the day of Pentecost. Jesus' leaving was a blessing, a true ministry of absence.

I had two friends in the deepest of crises, and I knew they were both depending too much on me and not enough on Jesus. So I made the difficult choice of making myself scarce for a time, entering into a ministry of absence. What did that look like for me? It meant that I did not answer the phone every time they called. I did not respond to emails or texts. Whenever I would see one of their names on my caller ID or in a text, I would pray fervently that they would go to Jesus and ask Him to clarify things for them and comfort them. This ministry of absence—removing my voice and my "omnipotence"— provided a context where the silence allowed each woman to actually hear the holy whisper of the Spirit within them. Of course the Junior God Badge part of me struggled to be silent and still, but the results were remarkable. I wish I had learned about this ministry of absence sooner—but this wannabe omnipotent was fueled by too much fear, insecurity, and pride.

In an interview in *Leadership Journal*, Pastor Bill Hybels discussed the secret of "strategic neglect." He mentioned that learning this principle was critical for "uncluttering" the soul. "Uncluttering the soul" sounded very appealing to this exhausted, controlling woman, and the phrase "strategic neglect" made me think of the ministry of absence. He remarked: "When you get the laser focus on exactly what God wants you to do, then travel lightly, and strategically neglect things you aren't called to do. You'll feel less rushed, and you'll slowly lose that chronic anxiety that you left something undone."[10] (I recommend Hybel's book, *Simplify: Ten Practices to Unclutter Your Soul.*)

If you and I are to walk free of the chronic anxiety common to all Junior God Badge wearers, we need to learn about strategic neglect as well as the ministry of absence. We will revisit the application of these critical principles with more detail in the ninth chapter.

DISCUSSION QUESTIONS

1. Why do you think Christian women seem to be graded on an unrealistic scale? Does a Christian woman have to be "omnipotent" to fulfill this high standard? (See Colossians 3:23.)

2. Are you the family idol? Review what an idol is: "Whenever I let someone draw their happiness or peace from me, I am an idol." Are you an idol in a friend's life? If you are, how do you feel about it?

3. Consider the danger of being anyone's idol. How have you learned to strategically neglect those who would make you an idol? Remember: "Those who cling to worthless idols forfeit the grace that could be theirs" (Jon. 2:8). "Little children, keep yourselves from idols" (1 John 5:21 NKJV).

4. How may you have allowed others to put God's crown on your head? Have you visualized your name sharing the marquee with God? (See Hebrews 4:15-16.)

5. How, in your omnipotence, might you have become an emotional paramedic at home, work, and church? (See John 3:30; Exodus 14:14.)

6. Discuss the expression, "ministry of absence."
    Are you ready to pull away and let the Holy
    Spirit work in your loved one's heart? (See
    John 16:7.)

CHAPTER 5

WANNABE OMNISCIENT

The motivation behind the controlling woman is always fear, insecurity, and lack of self-esteem. In order to control her world, she tries to be omniscient, which means having infinite awareness and understanding. Which, of course, is impossible.

That doesn't stop her from trying, though. The wannabe omniscient woman strives to understand all the information that comes her way so that she can better control the lives of the people in her world. She reads, studies, and attends seminars. Unfortunately, too often she may become an "emotional bully" in her church or family in her passionate attempt to persuade those around her of her superior point of view. I know because I have spent hours counseling young moms and wives who have been thoroughly intimidated by some woman they know from a local mom's group or Bible study.

The insecurity of these women allows them to be easy prey for the all-knowing control freak. It doesn't matter that the all-knowing woman's comments are simply her opinion or preference, and that those around her do not need to take them on as their own.

When I was a young mom, almost every Bible study group I attended had one of these omniscient women trying to bully all of us into conformity to her view of God's perfect guidelines for motherhood or whatever. One time a young mother stomped out of my house in an absolute rage because I had disagreed with the parenting style that she had embraced as having been delivered to earth from heaven. As she skidded out of our driveway, I knew that life would teach her that there is no one-size-fits-all formula for parenting. But it took a while. Years later (because by God's grace we remained friends), she asked me, "Why didn't you say something to me?!"

I replied, "I tried. And I have skid marks in my driveway to prove I tried!" This woman was an intimidating wannabe omniscient deity, and she left many victims behind in her dust. My "recovering deity's" heart was guarded, because I had learned the limitations on what I could control in the lives of those I love.

In this day and age, we have a new domain in which the wannabe omniscient can reign. Social networking is full of omniscient women trying to let everyone know *the* way to do life, whether that means how to decorate for your child's first birthday or throw the perfect baby shower. Seriously, listen, I love to look at decorating ideas as much as the next gal, but when the presentation becomes compulsive and demanding, it makes me recoil. This advice about what's "perfect," "best," and "right" becomes nothing but a noose of bondage for other insecure women.

Recently, a precious mommy-to-be was explaining her "birth plan" for their baby, and I had to take a few deep breaths and kept my opinion to myself. I have nothing against birth plans, but when they get down to what color nail polish the obstetrician should wear or whether the midwife is gluten-free...well, you get my point. Every generation of new mommies thinks it knows more than the older mommies!

The omniscient wearer of the Junior God Badge is often pretty startled when her incredible formula fails. What? My child did not turn out as wonderful as the formula promised he would? She fails to realize that there has only been *one* perfect child ever—and it was Jesus, who cannot have any peers.

I didn't have social networking to intimidate me as a young mom, but I clearly remember the wannabe omniscient advice-givers of my young-mom days. They seemed to know it all. Coming from a non-believing background, I was extra-vulnerable to the opinions of these Christians, assuming they must know better that I did, because I was raised only with religious traditions, not biblical values and insights.

CONFERENCE FEVER

Because I lacked a Christian upbringing, I dove right into being a wannabe omniscient deity myself, with incredible passion. Before I got married, I went to all of the marriage seminars, working at the registration desk so I could sneak in and learn everything about marriage. Before I got pregnant and had kids, I had already read every book I could find on parenting and I was attending all of the conferences for parents who wanted to raise their kids to be happy and holy. Why did I knock myself out to learn so much? Because I thought if I could only know *everything* about making a husband and kids happy while God made them holy, I would never make the mistakes I had witnessed in so many broken marriages and messed-up families.

Now I am not only a conference attender but a seasoned conference speaker, and I have grown along the way. But over the years I have learned how to *savor* the nourishment God gives me at a conference—not to so frantically devour it! I no longer "binge" on conference material, trying to bulk-up my omniscience. Instead, I ask the Lord to give me glimpses of *His* omniscience in the variety of ideas that are shared. After all, the benefit of conferences and books on different topics such as marriage and parenting is to appreciate that variety of offerings and then see what to assimilate and what to disregard as not a good fit.

GOOD BAD EXAMPLES

When a young guy committed adultery in a very new marriage, my friends and I were almost rabid in our effort to understand how in the world such a wonderful Christian couple could let this breach occur in their covenant relationship. Constantly, I was asking questions such as, "What do you think caused it?" "What do you think preceded the affair?" "What do you think led up to that?" I even spent part of the summer reading a very lengthy book about the mind of the adulterer.

One time at a home Bible study, a group of us were discussing our shock and despair about what had happened. Once again, we were asking our typical questions: "Why?" "How could this happen?" and an older woman in the room who mentors all of us spoke up: "I know why!" Silence. We all looked at her expectantly (drum roll!). Then this wise older woman simply said, "You know, the bottom line in adultery is two people are willing to sin together at the same time." Whereupon she added, "You girls can analyze it all you want. It's just sin."

Her words rang perfectly true, and I started to think about how women spend so much time trying to figure everything out. Some of us go around thinking that we already have figured it all out. It goes back to the reason Eve first touched the tree. Eve reached out toward the tree of the knowledge of good and evil because Satan told her that it could be a source of information that had been kept back from her. Satan appealed to Eve's desire to acquire knowledge that she had been deprived of: The wannabe omniscient woman reasons that if she has all of the knowledge of good and evil then she won't make the terrible mistakes that others are making in their marriage or in parenting. To avoid making mistakes guarantees that she can avoid pain, and avoiding pain is one of the fundamental motives of our independent, self-protective selves. With my thirst for omniscience, I actually acquired a good skill. I learned from other people's bad examples. I would ask people the "why" behind their choice and listen to the steps that led to the bad choice. Then, in the journal of my heart I would record, "Don't do what Marsha B. did!" I would thank people in my mind for the warning of their "good" bad examples. It was a privilege to have older people share with me their regrets and bad choices, and I learned from their sincere warnings. I had a friend who committed adultery, and she asked me to warn young women that the other side of adultery is pure hell. She wept when she shared the high price tag of the adultery in her life. I wept with her and thanked her for the warning and thanked her for allowing me to warn others.

For good reason, Paul warned us:

> *Run from sexual immorality! "Every sin a person can commit is outside the body." On the contrary, the person who is sexually immoral sins against his own body. Don't you know that your body is a sanctuary of the Holy Spirit who is in you, whom you have from God? You are not your own, for you were bought at a price. Therefore glorify God in your body* (1 Cor. 6:18-20, HCSB).

TRYING TO TRACE GOD'S PATH

One thing about striving to be an omniscient woman is the flaw of thinking you could ever have enough wisdom and insight to control your small part of the universe.

Taking a little time to consider how God's wisdom is described should be quite sobering for the omniscient woman: "Oh, the depth of the riches both of the wisdom and knowledge of God! How unsearchable His judgments and untraceable His ways! (Rom. 11:33, HCSB)

His wisdom is described as unsearchable, untraceable, past finding out. That means you can't trace it or figure it out. Yet the wannabe omniscient woman is intent on trying to figure out God's unfathomable ways and paths. God reiterates the facts:

> My thoughts are completely different from yours, says the Lord. And My ways are far beyond anything you could imagine. For just as the heavens are higher than the earth, so My ways are higher than your ways and My thoughts higher than your thoughts (Isa. 55:8-9, NLT).

Do you remember as a kid when you would use tracing paper to copy a picture? You would line up the tracing paper and do your best not to move the paper so the tracing was just perfect! Nothing was more frustrating than getting things all lined up…and then the paper moved. Groan! I think most Junior God Badge wearers spend their days trying to trace God's path and plan, groaning every time the paper moves. As Christians we are supposed to walk by faith, not by sight—and this is a profound challenge to a wannabe omniscient woman. Here are some wise words from a young wannabe omniscient named Esther Marion Fleece:

I'm learning that "winning" to God means *relationship*...and that makes me love Him even more. It's almost a gift when our life formulas don't work out (as crushing as it feels). It forces us to wrestle with God, and He can handle it. Hopefully I come out with a deeper understanding (and a clearer picture) of who He really is. He doesn't fit our formulas, He doesn't have our timing, and He's not subject to meeting my formulas or fixing my circumstances. And truthfully, at thirty-one years old, I'm just beginning to see His delays, His challenges and His pruning as a way He's saving me from me. I thought He was mean—turns out He's really kind. He has never left me. He is all I need.

The woman who wants to be omniscient usually has a library of books that are the foundation of all her formulas for life. She quotes incessantly from them. I wrote a book titled, *The Mentoring Mom*, and it is a compilation of all the principles I learned as my kids were growing up. I never intended the book to be a list of formulas; it was simply my heart in print concerning what I had learned from reading literally hundreds of books. I even put my book list in the back of the book. I not only read books, but I was constantly asking questions of older women about their marriages as well as their parenting styles. I always assumed I simply had a teachable heart, which is true, but I can't deny that some of my passion was fueled by my Junior God Badge. I remember as a baby Christian reading a book titled *Ten Steps to Christian Maturity*. I read that book several times, because I wanted to know the steps and make sure I was following them exactly. Talk about a formula-framed foundation! I had steps for my Christian walk and steps for making my husband happy and many steps for trying to shape my children into lovers of Jesus. All too easily, the omniscient woman begins to trust in "the formula" more than her brilliant Papa God.

As I have gotten older, I have come up with some unique advice for young women who are following a certain formula for creating a happy and holy family. What is this unique advice? Buy a seatbelt for yourself! Why? Because you're going to need a seatbelt to keep from getting *whiplash* when you have to slam on your brakes as you skid down the highway of disillusionment after your formula-driven life doesn't produce what you assumed it would. Striving to be an omniscient woman is an endless marathon, but the sweat is not so holy.

I wonder if we as women have always skipped over the "reality" Scriptures about wisdom, such as this one: "For with much wisdom comes much sorrow; the more knowledge, the more grief" (Eccles. 1:18). My husband found a companion verse for this reality of knowledge and grief. Eight little words, but they are a loud reminder of the "burden" of seeing: "The burden which the prophet Habakkuk saw" (Hab. 2:1, NKJV).

I have seen this situation often: A group of devoted Christian women find out that a certain woman followed a specific formula while raising her kids, and her kids turned out wonderfully well. So, the other mothers in her life assume because *their* kids are not necessarily so wonderful, it must simply be because they did not know the correct formula. I used to be jealous of a woman who appeared to have the greatest kids. People would talk about their awesome family, and I wondered what their secret was. This performance-based, perfectionistic household was very impressive. Years later when the lives of the children fell apart, I couldn't help but think of the reality that life is simply not guaranteed by a formula you follow. If it was, you would think that God would have followed a formula in the Garden with Adam and Eve. If He had one, it failed.

THE DESIGNER'S INTENT: DEPENDENCE RATHER THAN INDEPENDENCE

Here's a truth that is hard for some people to hear: God knows it is not for our good to get life all figured out, because then we will live independently of Him. We will think we can face each day in our own unfathomable wisdom. He doesn't want me to have how to be a great parent all figured out. He doesn't want me to have it all figured out how to be a great wife. Such comprehensive wisdom would allow me to become an independent version of Proverbs 3:5-6, and as a Junior God Badge owner I would have to devise a different translation of this common proverb. My version would be: "Trust in your *own* heart and lean on your *own* understanding and in all your ways acknowledge your own omniscience and direct your own path."

We pridefully train our families to trust in *us* with all their heart and not to lean on their own understanding but let Mama direct their path. Mama knows best. The wannabe omniscient mama prides herself in her unfathomable wisdom. She is like a walking Wikipedia! She sees herself as the capable, virtuous wife and mother as described in the following passage. "She speaks with wisdom, and faithful instruction is on her tongue" (Prov. 31:26).

We wives and mothers need to seek the Lord for wisdom, because we will never be the ultimate source for hope and direction! Being a wise mother doesn't mean being able to explain all the wonders of the world. I was so desperate to be omniscient so I could guide my children through the landmines of life. This omniscient mentality resulted in overkill. Not only did I overload my own kids with information, but I inundated any young person who came within a few feet of me! I would share information prematurely, in hopes of shielding those I love from hurt, disappointment, and heartache. Oh, the emotional and spiritual ills I caused through my premature information-sharing and my overkill sermons. This wannabe omniscient did not realize for years that *where my wisdom ends, God-dependency begins.* "For You have been my hope, Sovereign Lord, my confidence since my youth. From birth I have relied on You; You brought me forth from my mother's womb. I will ever praise You" (Ps. 71:5-6).

The earlier your loved ones learn passionate God-dependency, the better for them and for you! I spent too much of my life as an over-parenting helicopter mama, because I had assimilated so much information about raising happy and holy children. I assumed that I knew what was best for our children and what would keep them from heartache. However, as I have noted, I have come to see that over-parenting causes real emotional and spiritual ills. I have met so many young people who have struggled with the emotional ills of anxiety and depression, and too many of these young people came from Christian homes where the parents were as overbearing as I was as a wannabe omniscient way. Trying to run the show for someone else's life undermines his or her own sense of capability, which is just one of the ways kids become anxious when they have such parents: Without the safety net of Super Mom in every situation, they are always second-guessing if what they're doing is right or good enough. Failures, even minute ones, can cripple the offspring of wannabe omniscient moms.

I know that I was not the only parent who failed in this way, but I am now owning up to it in print: I was an omniscient helicopter parent who tried to be a super-guardian of my children. I was constantly taking my kids' spiritual temperature in an attempt to gauge how they were doing spiritually. ("How many times this week did you have your quiet time?") Such obsessive attention actually helped stifle the spiritual appetite of one of my kids; it produced a spiritual anorexic.

Even if my intention came from a protectiveness that I assumed was from deep love, my extreme parenting was harmful. I have apologized to both of our adult children for over-parenting them. They both have received my blessing to seek healing from the damage done by the Junior God Badge owner they had for a mama.

In regards to this dynamic, a friend of several adult children wrote to me:

> In the last couple of years, God has really worked in my heart and my husband's about this adult kid stuff. Even though I could get all worked up about some of my adult kids' current choices, I have unexpected peace. It isn't the best, but trust me it could be *far* worse. I actually get excited about what God can do with where they are right now. Mainly, I feel blessed we are all very close— in spite of it all. I am joyful they still come to us, want to be with us, share so many heart issues with us. They don't need our constant judgment, condemnation, exhortation, etc. I feel God has taken our hands away and said, "*Enough.* Your job is to love them, pray for them, and live your life in obedience. It is time for you *trust Me* to pursue their hearts. Their stories are not turning out the way you would have liked them to be written, but the end of the story is not done. I will go after my child. Trust me to be big enough."

SNOOPERVISING

As if over-parenting my children were not enough, as an omniscient wannabe I have also engaged in the sinful practice of "snoopervising." I made the word up, of course, but I think it is the perfect word for a woman who trespasses into God's territory in the lives of others. Let me explain. The omniscient woman thinks that with enough information people can be restrained from doing evil. The snoopervising omniscient woman is constantly getting involved in the lives of others with the intent and agenda of keeping people from making unwise choices. She assumes if she gives these precious people just enough information, transformation will be inevitable and evil will be averted. We're always so surprised when a knowledgeable man sins sexually. Why? He's just a man who sins. Why do we think that *information* will prevent people from doing evil? It won't. God might use information to jump-start us toward obedience, along with a little bit of faith. We're supposed to read His Word, not so much to get information as to get to know Him, and to ignite and strengthen our faith. It takes *faith* to obey God, not piles of facts and information. This is especially true when it comes to wanting to control other people, because it takes faith to keep your mouth closed when you'd love to tell a person how to live better.

Take a look at the lifestyle of the wisest man who ever lived, King Solomon. In First Kings chapter 3, God appears to Solomon in a dream and asks Solomon, "What do you want?" Solomon's reply is, "All I want is wisdom to lead these people." So God gives him more wisdom than anybody else. Now Solomon has a super intellect that would challenge Einstein or Stephen Hawking. But did his wisdom keep him from evil in his personal life? No! This man had four hundred wives and three hundred concubines—seven hundred women! Talk about wisdom being neutralized.

So what does this all have to do with snoopervising? Stay with me. The omniscient woman sprinkles her wisdom over anyone in her home (like watering a garden—although sometimes I was more like a fire-hose with my sharing of wisdom) and then she goes outside her home looking for others to bless and sprinkle with her wisdom—which puts her within a specific biblical boundary: "If you suffer, it should not be as a murderer or thief or any other kind of criminal, or even as a meddler" (1 Pet. 4:15). Peter is comparing a meddler to a criminal! I remember the first time I read this passage. I was flabbergasted that being a "busybody" was the same as being a murderer or a thief! Seriously? I decided to look up the definition of "meddler," and I found equivalents such as *busybody* and *superintending some else's household*. Ouch!

Snoopervising is *not* the same as encouraging, even if those of us who wear our Junior God Badges too often try to play God in the lives of others. We are only trying to be helpful, aren't we? …As we try to become the superintendent of someone else's house or someone else's life! My mentor Bettye Galbraith has warned me many times about snoopervising; she calls it a waste of my limited day-pass that I have here on earth.

So, why does Peter lock up busybodies in the same cell as murders and thieves? Peter is making the point that there are heart issues the meddler and the murder have in common. Murder and stealing are consummately selfish acts that are rooted in the most heinous pride. Someone is saying, "I want you gone, and you're gone! I want your belongings, so I'm just taking them." To superintend someone else's life says, "I know best," and by extension, "you're not capable. In fact, *God* is not capable." The foundation of meddling is also *pride*—and Peter is shaking up his readers by putting it on the same level as what we would consider serious crime, just as Jesus did! (Jesus compared being angry at a brother with murder in Matthew 5:22.) The wannabe deity deludes herself that she's acting out of love, but condescension and judgment—usual hallmarks for the busybody's mindset—have none of God's love as their motive.

Something that has really helped me to stop snoopervising other people's lives is to pray without ceasing (see 1 Thessalonians 5:17). If you have prayed faithfully about a concern for someone else's household, when that person asks you for wisdom, then you will be prayed up and you won't have to pin on your Junior God Badge to administer your ever-so-valuable wisdom. Your response will be humble and prayer-saturated wisdom from God (see James 1:5). If, on the other hand, they never ask for your help, prayer will give you the peace to yield their situation to the Lord. (Sometimes when I am tempted to snoopervise, I hear the warning, "Mind your own business, Jackie!")

One more deterrent for the snoopervisor woman: *It is not about you!* Once again, I had to learn this the hard way. One time, I was kept out of the "information loop" of a struggling friend, and I took it hard. I decided to process my frustration with my favorite Christian counselor and friend, Kathy Martin, after weeks of grieving as if I had betrayed. I told her how many years this friend and I have not only shared ministry privileges but our private worlds and struggles. Two decades of being BFFs, and this friend was going through the greatest trial, and I was not privy to any details. All this might sound ridiculous to a loner, but to a passionate people person like me, "lifer" friend that I am, it was devastating. For years I had been included in her inner circle and I had seen her through many heartbreaking times.

After telling my counselor all of my history with this friend, she asked, "Do you know why you are so upset?"

I nodded, "Yes. Because I have been treated unlovingly by a dear friend...isolated...left out...excluded."

Kathy said, "No. That is not why you are upset. *Your pride* is why you are upset. Your *pride* has made this seem like it's all about *you* and not about the deep struggle your friend is undergoing right now."

I just about fell out of my seat! *Pride?* I was already feeling hurt and rejected and now I was being told I was *proud?* I was too surprised to protest verbally, and you can imagine such silence is rare for this all-knowing omniscient wannabe. So I just listened to her explanation of how pride always makes everything seem to be about us, and we miss the actual reality. What is that reality? My dear friend is in pain, and she needs my compassion, not my self-centered need for inclusion nor my prideful assumption that I am entitled to be included.

I had asked for advice, and Kathy had supplied it. Now I needed to remember the verse that goes like this: "Let the godly strike me! It will be a kindness! If they correct me, it is soothing medicine. Don't let me refuse it" (Ps. 141:5, NLT). Since that day with Kathy, I have learned to ask myself, "Am I making this be about *me*, or am I focusing on finding the *loving reality* that I am called to walk in?" (See Philippians 2:3-5.)

As it happens, I am presently surrounded by suffering people, and I genuinely want to help and know what is going on, but I no longer want to try to frantically push my helpful self into every situation. Moreover, I no longer presume that I'm entitled to be in that inner circle of information. Having taken off my Junior God Badge, now I am praying and quietly waiting for a holy nudge and God's gentle permission to enter. For the snoopervising woman, this principle is hard to remember and implement. I have to keep telling myself, "It is not about me! I am not 911 Jackie!" I sure hope you have a couple of friends who love you enough to give you a "godly strike," like a bucket of ice water in your face to bring you out of the illusion of control. I have several women who love me enough to "strike" me—and they seem to need to do it on a regular basis. (These godly women know who they are!)

TWO COLLIDING OMNISCIENT WOMEN

Wannabe omniscients can't get along with each other, by and large, but it's not an unusual situation, nor is it a modern problem only. Consider Euodia and Syntyche in the Bible, who must have been two of the most passionate know-it-all women of all time, because their names are immortalized in Scripture. These two women were arguing, and their contentiousness was impacting the church. Can you imagine the greatest New Testament writer calling you out for arguing? Paul did not simply allude to some conflict between two unnamed women; he listed their names. Yikes!

Euodia and Syntyche served on a great Gospel team, and they had their names in the Book of Life, yet they *could not agree.* How sad to think that these women did not get only their "fifteen minutes of fame" but *centuries* of fame for being disagreeable. I looked this passage up in several translations and came across this in the Living Bible paraphrase:

> *And now I want to plead with those two dear women, Euodias and Syntyche. Please, please, with the Lord's help, quarrel no more—be friends again. And I ask you, my true teammate, to help these women, for they worked side by side with me in telling the Good News to others; and they worked with Clement, too, and the rest of my fellow workers whose names are written in the Book of Life.* (Phil. 4:2-3, TLB).

Can you imagine Paul having to waste one word on two quarreling women? Can you imagine Paul having to ask his Gospel team to help these women stop quarreling? I realize that I am particularly sensitive to the impact of this passage, and I see it as a screaming reminder to me to behave in a godly way. *I do not want to be famous for quarreling with a sister-in-Christ.* Instead, I want to be known as a helpful "tag-team" member for the Gospel.

Euodia and Syntyche's argument is recorded for us in the biblical record to make it even more clear that arguing and whining are not acceptable; along with stubborn resistance to correction, they are linked to the need to control others. The wannabe omniscient woman believes her deep wisdom should not be challenged—even by one of the greatest Christians who ever lived. Are you teachable, or are you so rigid that your biographical sketch is going to read like that of Euodia or Syntyche?

I decided to look up the meaning of the names *Euodia* and *Syntyche*, and I was intrigued.

Euodia means "a good, brave, noble way" and Syntyche means "friendly and easy to talk to." Now, obviously these two girls were not living up to their names! This is a great illustration of the unfortunate way that control undermines the noble aspect of a woman. As a woman strives with others over her right to be right, she will often forfeit her true, God-given identity.

Are you ready to remove your Junior God Badge and cease striving to display your unfathomable wisdom? Are you ready to be more God-dependent than formula-dependent? Are you ready to have the "omniscient" title removed from your bio? Can you cease striving to achieve perfect parenting? Can you stop searching for *the* method for being the perfect wife? Clarifying disclaimer: God has used many books in my life, and I often see books as a way of getting to know my brothers and sisters in Christ. I can't meet with Elisabeth Elliot, for example, but I can sit down with a cup of coffee and one of her books, and it is like having a mentoring moment with an older godly woman. I believe that we become the sum total of what we have read, and that reading the Bible daily is a must. However, I no longer read looking for formulas or methods to control everything. I read to be encouraged and to look for hope for my soul and the souls of others.

> *The Sovereign Lord has given me a well-instructed tongue, to know the word that sustains the weary. He wakens me morning by morning, wakens my ear to listen like one being instructed* (Isa. 50:4).

DISCUSSION QUESTIONS

1. How do you think that your thirst for knowledge flows from the desire to control your universe—especially the lives of your loved ones? (See Jeremiah 9:23-24.)

2. Discuss the impact of social networking on a woman's ability to be omniscient (confidently all-knowing). (See Proverbs 21:30.)

3. How often do you read books in search of formulas to help you trace God's path for you and your loved ones? (See Isaiah 55:8-9; Romans 11:33.) Are you a "formula woman"?

4. Do you have a friend who has become disillusioned when her formula-driven life didn't produce what she assumed it would? (Remember, formulas do not require you to walk by faith.) (See Ecclesiastes 1:18; Hebrews 11:6.)

5. How might you have been like this Junior God Badge owner, who did not realize for years that *where my wisdom ends, God dependency begins?* (See Psalm 71:5-6.)

6. Discuss the seriousness of "snoopervising." (See 1 Peter 4:15.) Does it surprise you that "snoopervising" can be compared with criminal behavior?

7. Does it bother you that two women who loved Jesus were cited in the Bible because of their arguing? Wannabe omniscient women are often stubbornly set on their viewpoints. (See Philippians 4:2-3.)

CHAPTER 6

WANNABE JEHOVAH-SHALOM

The next characteristic of some Junior God Badge owners may not be as obvious as others. This wannabe deity can actually be particularly soft-spoken and sweet. Her placid demeanor can fool people, even herself! This is the woman striving to be like Jehovah-Shalom, the God of peace (see Judges 6:24; *shalom* is the Hebrew word for peace). She has a dysfunctional sense of responsibility about the feelings of others. She learns how to tread very cautiously, dodging anger and conflict, and directing others to carefully dodge the anger landmines around them. As I was growing up, my mother constantly directing me and my siblings in how not to upset Dad. We became experts at tiptoeing through the landmines of his anger—and then other people's—moods. One characteristic of a landmine-dodger? She's very flexible. I learned to wrap myself around like a pretzel, bending and twisting and flexing to keep peace at any price. As a contortion artist, however, the wannabe Jehovah-Shalom is always paying the bill emotionally.

Countless women spend their whole lives walking around on eggshells, trying to keep peace at any price, instructing their children in very specific behaviors lest they upset Daddy or another relative of influence. I have spent too much of my life walking on eggshells around certain family members. It grieves me to say that I never unlearned eggshell walking until I became an adult. Through serious counseling, I came to learn the danger of trying to keep peace at any price, and it wasn't the eggshells breaking. The wannabe Jehovah-Shalom mom teaches her children to walk on eggshells, and they soon learn that peace at "any price" means that *they* must pay the price! Children learn to live a lie, hiding their pain behind polite smiles. They become adults who are trained to be polished pretenders in order to keep the peace.

When I was in ninth grade at James Madison High School, I won an award for having the best smile. I was fifteen years old, living in an abusive home where my dad was coming through a window at night to get into my locked bedroom—yet I had the "best smile." I had already entered the training school of looking full and fine when in reality I was empty and broken. This is what the wannabe Jehovah-Shalom woman trains her children: "Look full when you are empty. Look happy when you are sad." She trains them in proper external behavior even when it absolutely does not match their hearts. After these well-trained children go off to college, how surprised the parents are when their offspring don't behave as they were trained to do! The grown children finally stop doing the "Eggshell Two-Step" (also commonly known as the "Christian Two-Step"). The controlling woman will blame college for this lapse in the life of her child. Actually, however, college only reveals what's really there in the young person's heart. It's a painful truth for Mrs. Junior God that she can only control a child who lives under her jurisdiction. (And because of this, I know mothers who would seriously consider going *with* their kids to college, just to keep him or her under her influence!)

FAMILY PUNCHING BAG

The Jehovah-Shalom woman takes "Blessed are the peacemakers" (Matt. 5:9) to an extreme, avoiding confrontation at all cost. She runs interference between her children and their father—triangulating every conflict or miscommunication—always explaining the behavior of the father to his kid or the kid to the father. Of course, the father and child can't get to know each other because of the ever-present Jehovah-Shalom wannabe interfering with their need to work through conflict. One time when I was trying to mediate between Ken and the kids, Ben said something to me that almost tore off my Junior God Badge right in that moment. "Mom, aren't you tired of being the family punching bag?" Ouch! Then he said, "I think that 'peacemakers' are really the family's punching bag." His comments ended whatever mediation I thought

I was going to expedite that evening. It caused me to begin to consider the painful reality of his remarks.

I have a friend whose husband is often upset with their son. Rather than expressing his disappointment directly to his son, he vents his frustration to his wife. Then she goes and *calmly*, Jehovah-Shalom-style, expresses to her son his father's disappointment with his carelessness or selfishness or whatever. Commonly, the son will explain why he seemed careless, and to the mother it makes perfect sense. But when Mom goes to explain it to Dad, something is always lost in the translation. Now Mom is perplexed, Dad is still frustrated, and the greatest thing that has been lost in this scenario is the chance for father and son to forge a deeper relationship through heart-to-heart communication. What Junior Jehovah-Shalom couldn't tolerate was the possibility that some of the talking could be laced with frustration and disappointment. So, instead, while these two have lived under the same roof, they have only learned to be emotionally estranged from each other—while Mom continues to be loved by both of the men in her life.

This particular friend finally learned to direct each man in her life to speak to the other one, rather than using her as the peacemaking mediator. She learned to move out of the middle and to challenge the men to express their frustration to one another and to reason together. She shared with me her regret for not getting out of the middle sooner! I reminded her that the Junior God Badge wearer always assumes she knows best for her child. Ironically, women are inclined to criticize their husbands for not really understanding their children, yet it's hard to get to know one's child when Mama Shalom is standing in front of the child as a shield.

Do you need to get out of the middle of the relationship between your husband and children? Do you need to lay down your title as Head Counselor and Mediator? If you do, ask the Lord for His grace to do what is right. Retiring from being Jehovah-Shalom requires great bravery for all involved.

It's a paradox that this woman does not actually bring about peace or experience peace, because she is always anxiously, busily mediating, explaining, and acting like a public defender for each of her family members. Peace is so far from her reach! "You will keep the mind that is dependent on You in perfect peace, for it is trusting in You" (Isa. 26:3, HCSB).

I want to point out that it's not only married women who are wannabe Jehovah-Shaloms. This exact same dynamic can take place among a group of friends or in the workplace. Daughters and nieces can take this role in their families. A gal does not need a ring on her left hand to qualify as the self-appointed Super Mediator. The only symbol she needs is her Junior God Badge. So, no matter what your status is, please get honest about your membership in this club and be careful about being Jehovah-Shalom for your family or friends. The Scripture states that God provides perfect peace for the person who is dependent on *Him*, not dependent on herself. The Word also encourages us to let the *peace of Christ* rule in our hearts, not the peace of Jehovah-Shalom Junior (see Colossians 3:15).

We have to teach the people we love to go to God's Throne before they pick up the phone and call "911 Mom" or "911 Sister" or "911 Best Friend." In every crisis there will always be someone who comes to mind to call before a person cries out to God directly.

Just like the wannabe omnipresent, omnipotent, and omniscient woman, the Jehovah-Shalom woman has trained her loved ones to depend on her. Yet as I mentioned, this woman does not actually experience peace, because she is so consumed with orchestrating life for her loved ones that she ends up fatigued, drained, and depressed. No human can be god-like for others without running out of energy. A woman named Karen Jennings posted the following on Facebook:

> I have struggled for years with debilitating anxiety attacks. Then, after some key moments orchestrated by God, I saw the root cause was that I struggled with control. I wanted to control everything and everyone around me. I had an unbalanced view of God. I even joined a very legalistic cult where everything about life was very strictly drawn out for me.
>
> After I learned how much God loved me, I came to understand His sovereignty and I saw that nothing could come into my life that He did not allow and that nothing takes Him by surprise. I was terrified of dying, even as a Christian, but

God in His mercy showed me that as His child I will not take one less breath than He has planned for me. I can trust Him not only with my life but the lives of those around me. I am not responsible for the actions of others, but I am to pray and trust.

I feel like I am not communicating this well. But I thank God I am free from the bondage of trying to control.

HURRICANE WINDOWS FOR THE SOUL

In South Florida, we need to protect our houses during hurricanes. A very expensive form of protection is to install "impact-resistant" windows that can handle both small and large missiles of debris. People report watching wind-driven debris as it crashes into their impact-resistant windows, and the windows remain perfectly intact. It's important to protect the windows; we Floridians know that when the windows get blown out—there goes the house.

Recently, a dear friend has been in a brutal hurricane of the emotional variety—a category-5 storm, with emotional winds exceeding 157 mph. Thinking about her, I was reading Romans 15, and I got excited when I saw that "hurricane windows" are available for our souls in preparation for the storms that we will face. Just how can these impact-resistant windows get installed in our souls? "For everything that was written in the past was written to teach us, so that through the endurance taught in the Scriptures and the encouragement they provide we might have hope." (Rom. 15:4).

When you and I spend regular time reading the Scriptures, God installs these impact-resistant windows in your soul by means of the encouragement that is available. This friend of mine is not only surviving the storm, but she is clinging to Jesus with hope. Her preparation for her present storm occurred during the months and years she chose to make a priority of time spent with Jesus in His Word. Now her intentionality and faithfulness are on display, because the windows of her soul have remained intact in spite of the fact that her marriage has faced many assaulting missiles. Yes, the fierce winds are blowing and dangerous pieces of debris are slamming into her life, but her soul windows are still intact, and her hope remains.

Neglecting our time with Jesus in the Scriptures means that we will not be prepared for the hurricanes that are coming. The hurricanes will reveal our lack of "pre-storm prep." The wise proverb diagnoses the problem: "If you falter in a time of trouble, how small is your strength" (Prov. 24:10).

Tomorrow when you are considering not spending a little time in the Word, consider the possible "missile" that may be aimed at your soul's windows already. How does this relate to the Jehovah-Shalom woman? The most terrifying storm for her is to witness a disagreement between two people she loves. She starts breaking into a sweat as the disagreement becomes passionate, and the windows of her soul are in danger of breaking, too.

DANGEROUS TRIANGULATING

In yet another episode of "Jackie Plays Peacemaker," I inserted myself into a conversation between my son Ben and my husband Ken. I was explaining Ben's GPA to his father (as if his father couldn't possibly understand an academic grade point average) and also trying to tell our son what his dad meant by the statement he had just made. All it took was Ben's quizzical look to get me underway. I immediately jumped in, trying to explain and interpret both sides, in hopes of keeping things as smooth as possible. The wannabe Jehovah-Shalom woman, in her attempt to keep family peace, is always trying to water down or explain away a concern, especially one that is presented by her spouse. This woman so wants to avoid a confrontation at the dinner table or in the car that she regularly jumps in to defuse the "concerns" of her spouse.

Another version of this defusing of tensions is her compulsion to explain the less-than-perfect behavior of the father to the child. I grew up with a mom who constantly defended the less-than loving behavior of my father. I remember one time speaking up at the dinner table when my dad said something that was absolutely, on every continent, wrong. I did not scream or shout, but in my junior high voice I said, "Dad, that is not true." Well, my dad went ballistic, to say the least, and my peacemaker mother jumped in to try and defuse the eruption. He ranted for a few moments and then he calmed down, but what I remember best is how, later that night, my peacemaking mother said to me, "You need to learn to be quiet and not say things that upset your father!" The much-repeated stanza of our family song was, "Be careful—Don't upset your father!"

A sad consequence of the triangulating of a Jehovah-Shalom woman is that while she is getting in the middle between child and father, trying to pull them together, she is actually building a wall between them. This woman is not even aware that she is making daily trips to that construction site. Years later she is so sad that the child and father do not have a good relationship. Being the emotional mediator between one's children and spouse (or between any other parties, for that matter) seems to be a logical extension of a female skill. Women are better than men at fielding the emotional aspects of relationships. However, that does not mean they can assume that their emotional GPA gives them the *right* to mediate and triangulate between other people.

One evening I was doing dishes after one of my "triangulating sessions," and I clearly sensed that the Lord saying to me, "The badge is coming off; it's got to come off right now." then the Lord Himself showed me how my controlling tendency had just added a few more bricks to the wall between my husband and his child! I was not proud of myself. I knew I might need some heaven-sent duct tape to paste over my mouth to constrain me the next time I was tempted to get involved in a "lively discussion" between father and child.

When you act as a mediator between any two people, they may both end up loving you, but they never get to know each other because *you* are in the way. This means that any member of your family you are explaining to another member of your family, any member of your church committee you are regularly explaining to other members, anyone in your office, your neighborhood, the PTA…get the point? You need to find the exit and use it. Get out of the middle of their discussion (or lack of discussion).

I won't pretend for a minute this is an easy role to give up. There are deep reservoirs of anxiety and insecurity that feed this behavior. The Jehovah-Shalom woman gets nervous about giving up her role as peacemaking mediator because she loves being loved by everyone! She gets to be the "good guy" in these stressful situations. It is *very* uncomfortable for her to tolerate tension and conflict because, at some deep level, it says to her, *"This is not safe! Make it stop!"* If we look beneath the behavior, the motive that has likely fueled her for years is, once again, self-protection. If she thinks she can keep things calm and help people understanding each other, if she can be the good guy and secure their love and approval, then she can feel safe.

It's not only a hard role to give up, it can be difficult to see the fear that fuels it—especially because the outcome seems so righteous. God alone can reveal this to you, so please, if you are not already doing this, ask your heavenly Papa to show you what is really going on for you. Ask Him, too, for the peace in your heart to hold your tongue in situations you might habitually leap into. The Holy Spirit will enable you to stand there quietly—no matter what level of panic is screaming for attention inside your head—and just let the people do their thing. That might be yelling and it might be silence, but Jesus can work through any of it. Remember, God is standing ready to heal your heart and mind, so surrender to Him in this realm and see what He can do.

With the help of a heavenly muzzle, I learned to cease being the family's interpreter. If my husband has a question or my child has a question, I encourage them to go straight to the source. Years later, as I watch both my children dialogue with freedom with their dad, I am so glad I surrendered my Junior God Badge in this area. This peacemaker needed to retire so everyone could get to know each other and stop avoiding the challenges of interpersonal relationships.

Life is messy, relationships are messy. The wannabe Jehovah-Shalom needs to allow others to move at the pace they are capable of—and the pace God knows they are capable of. Your prayers are more effective than all of your hovering over others emotionally. If you are a mother, this is a crucial principle to learn before your children become young adults. *Crucial!* Interfering mothers produce emotionally crippled people who cannot thrive in a relationship that Mom is not mediating!

There is a prophecy in the book of Malachi that mentions turning the hearts of fathers toward their children and the hearts of children toward their fathers (see Malachi 4:5-6). Whenever I read this passage, I always reflect that the biggest challenge is to get "controlling mom" out of the way so that the relationship between fathers and children can be built. It could even be said that when a controlling mother allows her children to come to her for everything they need, she moves to a place of idolatry in their lives. Women may defend their need to mediate and be there 24/7 as mediator and controller (for the single mom, there may be no other option), but in fact, they are working to be in first place every time they run interference for another situation in the household. God alone is meant to be in first place.

DEFENSIVE MAMA AND SENSITIVE CHILD

Sometimes mothers will defend their controlling and peacemaking between a strong husband and a particularly "sensitive" child. They don't realize that their sensitive child might not need the hovering mother as much as he or she needs the strong and hard-to-relate-to father in order to grow emotionally stronger. A defensive mama stunts her children's growth by running interference between the child and life's tough challenges, whether in the home or outside the home.

If your sensitive child has a question for her father, let her ask the father. Even if your child is a little nervous to ask, home is the best place to practice doing what one is afraid to do, because home should be safe enough to handle potential conflict. Failure and fear are not fatal. I know moms who have pulled their son or daughter out of sports because a coach yelled at their child. Really? Life is full of people who do not speak in sweet decibels. Now the child will be handicapped if his or her first boss possesses a loud voice and a less-than charming management style.

The Jehovah-Shalom woman reads Matthew 5:9 ("Blessed are the peacemakers, for they will be called sons of God") and shouts, "See, when I am a peacemaker in my home, church, and community, I am demonstrating my true family of origin; I am a child of God!" The problem for the controlling woman, though, is that she doesn't differentiate between what *she does* to keep the peace and what the *Holy Spirit* does to bring about peace. True, He might borrow your voice for a specific moment of mediation in conflict, while allowing the Holy Spirit to keep you peaceful when others are agitated and wanting to argue. However, that's not the same as trying to control everyone in the room, or, even worse, seething in silent tension. A biblical peacemaker pushes people toward God and toward each other to work things out rather than pushing people to live in absolute dependence on her! Holy-Spirit-led peacemakers will promote reconciliation between people, rather than have them look to the peacemaker for everything.

I AM THE RECEPTIONIST, NOT THE DOCTOR

Almighty Mrs. Mediator needs to recognize the fact that she is the receptionist, not the doctor. Often our dysfunctional sense of responsibility causes us to believe that we are called to personally expedite the deep work in people's souls. It's not our job. The sanctification of a soul begins and ends with God (see John 17:17).

It can be shocking to a Jehovah-Shalom wannabe to discover that she is merely a receptionist and not the doctor. The receptionist is not responsible to fix people. The receptionist is responsible for making appointments and taking the patient's history, and that's about it. Her primary line is, "The doctor will see you in a moment." How bizarre it would be to walk into a doctor's office and witness the receptionist diagnosing a patient's health problem and then writing a prescription for the symptoms! Part of surrendering your Junior God Badge will be to remind yourself daily, "I am *the receptionist, not the doctor.*"

If only I had grasped this principle years ago! My own exalted sense of responsibility persuaded me that Jesus wanted me to bring peace and hope everywhere I went... including every party or social event I ever attended. I am embarrassed to admit that I have so few memories of great parties that I have attended since becoming a Christian. I would show up at every party wearing my Junior Omnipotent *and* my Junior Jehovah-Shalom Badges. It's as if I chose those badges so that I would be ready to arrest some woman's emotional drama. There could be twenty other capable women in the room, but I would be the one that the group would nudge into the crisis-corner to speak with the woman with tears pouring down her face. Why had none of these many concerned women already spoken to her when her tears began to fall? Because I had trained my gang so well to "wait for Jackie"—even if none of us quite realized that's what was happening.

When I began to grasp that I was not responsible for everybody's peace and hope, I was able to take off my Junior God Badge and allow someone else to speak to the weepy woman. It's interesting to note also that the others have changed accordingly throughout the years; the welcoming committee is no longer hovering at the door of a festivity, waiting to escort me to where the crisis is. Thank You, God, for the way we have all grown! Since I know that I am hardly the only one who was like this, I want to liberate other women from their peacemaking role. The many women in the body of Christ who feel obligated to attend to every mama drama they see end up missing valuable fellowship with other Christians. The only fellowship we get comes as we stand in the corner listening to someone's latest drama. We find it nearly impossible to hear God's voice of direction and correction in the midst of the outpouring of passion.

Early one morning, during a crazy summer storm, the thunder and lightning felt so near to the window I was reading next to that I almost moved my chair. As I continued to read and the storm raged on, I suddenly heard something startling in the midst of the thunderous noise. I actually heard the cooing of a dove. The rolling thunder and pounding rain did not drown out that dove's mild cooing. I couldn't see the dove, but I could hear it. This made me think of how we followers of Jesus can actually hear the "cooing" of the heavenly Dove in our storms—*if* we are listening carefully. I got excited as I thought about the many times I have heard the Holy Spirit's quiet remarks right in the middle of a horrific storm. How has this happened in your life? In the middle of the next storm you face, anticipate listening for the voice of the heavenly Dove "...who comforts us in all our troubles" (2 Cor. 1:4)

We need all the comfort and strengthening we can get, given our tendency to give in to fear in the middle of any storm. A woman named Celia Swink contributed the following email musing:

> My whole life I've been operating from a basis of fear and insecurity which has definitely caused me to be an overachieving perfectionist, bent upon minimizing the uncertainty, pain and risk in my life. However, I used to think that I was *not* one of those "controlling" people you hear about. What I didn't realize is that, although I'm not bent on controlling others, I spend every waking moment trying to control *myself* and my circumstances. I was controlling after all. Wow, what a realization!
>
> I'm thankful that God never thinks I'm too old to learn and that He continues to be merciful and patient with me! I prayed this morning for the first time that God would help me to recognize when I am in "independence" mode, and that little by little, hour by hour, day by day, I would start resting and *relaxing* in knowing that He has this amazing, wild love for me (like the kind I have for my son) and know He only wants the very best for me! Besides, I am only fooling

myself to think I am in control—I mean really! Last time I checked, I didn't have supernatural powers.

ANYONE WANT DESSERT?

Once in a while, a peacemaker is just what you need. Here's a story about a helpful peacemaker in a tense situation. A couple decades ago, I was leading a retreat in Stowe, Vermont. The group was composed of young wives who were mostly young Christians. An older woman joined the retreat for only one afternoon, and she stirred up trouble by bringing up a very controversial topic that I was not willing to discuss with such young believers. I actually had to tell the woman we would "take it outside" to resolve our argument. Right after I indicated that I would discuss it alone with her outside, with tension rising in the room, a young "peacemaker" suddenly spoke out and said, "Does anyone want some dessert?" Immediately the tension subsided as the women stood up to get some dessert! The little distraction was perfect for the situation.

My peacemaker friend and I laugh when we reminisce about how she averted a disastrous confrontation in front of so many young believers. I have always been grateful for her well-placed interruption. I think of it as a good example of this piece of wisdom found in the book of Proverbs: "A gentle answer turns away wrath, but a harsh word stirs up anger" (Prov. 15:1).

For so many years of my life as a Christian, I used to wish I could be one of those *nice* peacemakers like my friend. I liked how sweet and placid that kind of peace-maker always appeared. Of course as I have had the privilege of getting to know some of these women, and I have learned that these women can be Jehovah-Shalom wannabes, too. They find it very difficult to rock the boat, even when the boat needs to be rocked. Some of these women attended a Bible study with me, and I watched them learn how to speak up and not walk on eggshells. The Bible encourages us to speak the truth in love, but She Who Walks on Eggshells never feels the "time is right" for the truth to be expressed. These recovering eggshell-walkers have taught me so much about the courage to speak up (of course speaking the truth lathered with love). These recovering women are learning how to speak the truth even to someone who is struggling. They have come to see that tolerating (or simply deflecting attention from) bad behavior does not bless the one tolerated.

My great friend Kathy Martin constantly reminds me that it is a "sin" to smile when you are deeply hurt and too afraid to speak up! Peacemakers are too worried about what a person might think of them if they stated how that person's behavior was hurtful. The sin of their silence isn't in simply being quiet when someone hurts them. It is the resentment that can grow in their hearts in the face of unloving treatment. Peacemakers are pros at tolerating relational crimes, but below their quiet, peaceful exterior is often brewing a volcano of resentment! The peacemaker who internalizes everything will either die from a broken heart or a volcanic eruption. Sometimes instead of erupting all at once, it comes out as "volcanic depression and anxiety" in their lives. Recovering silent-type Jehovah-Shaloms need to be sure to learn the divine art of forgiveness, which will rescue them from much internal agony.

Being a Holy-Spirit-led peacemaker is wonderful, but the weakness of a former Jehovah-Shalom Junior will always be the inability to speak up when things are not truthful or are very hurtful. She defaults to avoiding confrontation of any kind. This woman will bear grief, endure lies, and suffer hurt rather than speak up and state the truth. The other reality about this woman's silence is that it reinforces her identity as a "victim." Not only does the unconfessed hurt too often fester into resentment, the dark side of the victim mentality is always our great nemesis, *pride.*

You see, the silent "victim" gets to maintain a kind of spiritual superiority over people who have (maybe unknowingly and completely unintentionally) hurt her. This can be almost too subtle to recognize, and she can become very invested in this subterranean identity. If this woman starts to stand up and speak up, her long-term identity will begin to crumble, and that is one of the things she is trying to avoid at all cost.

The peacemaker is always defined as being the good cop and never the bad cop. Recently I heard a mother say the she was always a good mom and the kids never gave her any trouble. Of course the kids never gave her any trouble—because she never gave them any grief! A mom who always says yes to the requests of her children will always be the "good" parent, the "fun" one. Unfortunately this kind of non-confrontational good parent raises children who will struggle all their lives as they encountered a world that is not so ready to say, "Yes. Sure. Whatever you want!"

The good news is that the genuine Jehovah-Shalom, God Himself, will walk with her as the "old man" dies away and the new creation emerges!

THE PRESUMPTUOUS JEHOVAH-SHALOM WOMAN

Like all versions of the Junior God, the Jehovah-Shalom woman can become totally unglued when life spills water all over her blueprints. This shows that a Jehovah-Shalom wannabe is often guilty of presumptuous sin. What's that supposed to mean? One aspect of presumptuous sin is pride's propensity to presume to know what's going to happen in the future. The Jehovah-Shalom woman wants to offer peace to those she loves by assuring them about what God will certainly do for them. She not only assumes that God will act in a certain way, she is equally confident in her ability to predict God-ordained outcome, repeatedly.

For example, I heard someone pray in a large group of people not too long ago, and I literally opened my eyes to see who it might be. This woman was thanking God that we can count on Him doing exactly as we have asked Him to do. She then exhorted the group in her prayer to not doubt that God will do what we ask. After the prayer time, she went up to the woman we were praying for and said, "I am sure God will do what we asked for."

The controlling woman is terrified that she might not get what she has prayed so hard for. She doesn't even consider the possibility that her blueprints might not get God's approval. Here is what God says about this:

> *Now listen, you who say, "Today or tomorrow we will go to this or that city, spend a year there, carry on business and make money." Why, you do not even know what will happen tomorrow. What is your life? You are a mist that appears for a little while and then vanishes. Instead, you ought to say, "If it is the Lord's will, we will live and do this or that." As it is, you boast in your arrogant schemes. All such boasting is evil. If anyone, then, knows the good they ought to do and doesn't do it, it is sin for them* (James 4:13-17).

Listen, I am all about asking God in faith for the things our souls long for and the things that those we love long for. But I also know that there are two perfect benedictions for all prayers. The first is what Jesus prayed, "Not my will but Thine be done" (see Luke 22:42). The second is what young Mary replied to the angel Gabriel, "Be it unto me according to Thy will, O Lord. I am Thy servant" (see Luke 1:38). A recognition of the presumptuous sin that fuels my scripts, my agenda, and my blueprints may be enough to motivate me to remove my Junior God Badge and replace it with a badge that boldly declares: *If it is the Lord's will.*

To all those who are clinging to their Junior God Badges and declaring boldly what they believe God is going to do, I would suggest reading the book of Job. Notice in the last chapter what God thought about Job's friends. They all spoke so spiritually, it seemed, yet all the while they were missing the truth about God. God was angered by Job's friends, and one of the accusations He made was, "They spoke of Me as of things that are not true" (see Job 42:7). All of us have heard people quote things they claim that God said, and I can assure you God did not say them. But they sound good—holy and powerful and spiritual—so they can get away with attributing the high sentiments to God. If you read the book of Job, you will notice that a lot of the things Job's friends said sound holy and spiritually impressive. Yet God was angry about the presumptuous statements they made.

We need to be aware of our human inclination to try to control God in prayer and to promise others what God will do. I suggest that we neither pray nor promise without adding something like "Lord willing." When I was a young Christian, I used to say "Lord willing" all the time, and then an older woman said to me, "You don't need to say, 'Lord willing' because that's understood."

That made me wonder, "If it's understood, how come nobody lives as if it's true?"

Much of the time, I would see women around me demonstrate a daily pattern of laying their agendas and plans for the day before the Lord, asking for His signature on her blueprints. We seem to be always telling God, "I want you to bless this thing I am going to do" or "I want you to be with me and give me wisdom *when* I do this." Such prayers only enlist God to cater to us in our self-directedness. You would have to call it self-worship. As such, it is like graffiti on the cross! Let God alone write your script.

Yes, do pray with faith and an expectant heart to see what God *will do*. Just be careful to let God be God, and avoid this presumptuous sin in prayer or testimony. When bold prayer is not answered according to the will of the person who prayed, people can end up discouraged and disillusioned with God. Is God the culprit? No, it's the one who prayed so presumptuously in prayer!

As an aid toward surrendering your Junior God Badge, I suggest that you get up in the morning, take a blank sheet of paper, and sign your name at the bottom. Let the Lord fill in His script and agenda for your day. There is always plenty of time each day for the will of God. Take that blank sheet of paper with you and put it somewhere you can see. Get ready for God to exercise total freedom to write the script for your day and to give you His peace as you execute His will, not yours.

"All the days ordained for me were written in Your book before one of them came to be" (Ps. 139:16).

UN-SNATCHABLE PEACE

One night I went to bed very early, because I was so tired in my soul as well as my body. I rose, still tired in my soul, needing to hear from Papa God. I always read God's Word anticipating some fresh insight. This particular morning that I was so needy and the Lord touched my soul so deeply that I cried in gratitude. "From eternity to eternity I am God. No one can *snatch* anyone out of my hand. No one can undo what I have done" (Isa. 43:13, NLT, emphasis added). As I cried and worshiped, the Lord gave me a new word: *un-snatchable*. I immediately thought of the New Testament version of this un-snatchable promise:

> *My sheep listen to my voice; I know them, and they follow Me.... And they will never perish. No one can* **snatch** *them away from me, for my Father has given them to me, and He is more powerful than anyone else. No one can* **snatch** *them from the Father's hand* (John 10:27-29, NLT, emphasis added).

These verses pumped such fresh oxygen into my weary soul that I was doing the "hamster dance" of joy when I finished my quiet time. What good news! Jesus provides this for those who believe in Him: an un-snatchable relationship with the King of Kings." May each of us tell the people in the crazy world around us that they too can have an *un-snatchable* relationship with the King of Kings!

The wannabe Jehovah-Shalom woman works so hard to keep the peace in her world that she is very often not full of peace herself. She is often anxious that a particular person is going to rob her of her peace—again. She may even decide to move out of her home in search of this elusive peace, but she never finds it, because peace is not part of a geographical location. Peace is the by-product of living in dependency upon the Prince of Peace, who is fully capable of keeping us close by His side forever.

DISCUSSION QUESTIONS

1. Statement: Too many women spend their lives walking around on eggshells trying to keep peace at any price. Do you agree or disagree? Why? (See Isaiah 26:3.)

2. The controlling woman is too often the family mediator. Is she also the family punching bag? Why can this be described as dangerous triangulating? (See 1 Timothy 2:5.)

3. Discuss: The peacemaker Mama can be a very defensive—especially on behalf of a sensitive child.

4. How might you feel overly responsible for the peace of everyone in the room? (See Philippians 4:7, Colossians 3:15.)

5. Who or what robs you of your peace, regularly? Discuss "Un-snatchable peace." (See Isaiah 43:13; John 10:17-29.)

6. Discuss the major challenge for a peacemaker: speaking painful truth that exposes who or what people trust in more than God. (See Proverbs 21:22.)

CHAPTER 7

WANNABE SOVEREIGN

Picture a gorgeously set Christmas table, ready for a family gathering. The hostess went all out this year when it came to decorating the dining room table. Even though she is better known for her cooking prowess than her decorating skill, this particular Christmas the hostess had a little extra time, so she decided to decorate as if Martha Stewart would be appraising her décor. The family arrives, and they immediately notice the beautiful table and comment on how wonderful it looks. Gifts are exchanged and opened; and when the hostess heads into the kitchen to turn on the oven, out of the corner of her eye she notices her son and daughter-in-law (very pregnant with their first child) going into the back room to make a call.

Suddenly the young couple emerges from the back room and states to the gathered family, "We need to get to the hospital, doctor's orders!" Everyone rushes around grabbing phones, purses, iPads, and the hostess stands watching the commotion with tears flowing. Hers are not tears because everyone is running out the door, but tears that her firstborn son will possibly have a baby girl on Christmas day. (Abigail was born that night at 8:13 P.M.)

Standing and looking at the beautifully decorated table, I asked my husband to take a picture. He asked why I wanted a picture of this empty table. I told him that I was going to put the picture of that empty Christmas table in my annual frame. (I have a picture from each Christmas since 1998). The picture will be a forever reminder of the one thing I can control in life—*my attitude* about what happens (see 1 Thessalonians 5:18). I learned a long time ago that I am simply not sovereign material.

SHE IS NUMERO UNO

The wannabe sovereign woman sees herself as the supreme volunteer, the personal assistant to *El Elyon*, the Most High God. But since the Sovereign of the universe is focused on so many needs, this woman assigns herself Head Chick in Charge to keep her corner of the universe from falling apart. Her motives may seem noble, but they are infused with such pride! Does she honestly think she could hold anything together in this crazy world? Yes. In her prideful heart, the wannabe sovereign thinks she's personal assistant *numero uno*. Yet the truth is unchanging: "He is before all things, and in Him all things hold together" (Col. 1:17).

Being a wannabe sovereign actually puts a woman in a battle with the ultimate sovereign of the universe. What will it take to persuade her of the truth? In the book of Revelation, the last book of the Bible, we read about Armageddon, where God and His enemies will gather for a final battle (see Revelation 16:16). I wonder if the controlling woman may have to end up in an Armageddon of a battle in order to finally surrender her Junior God Badge. Believe me, I have learned the hard way, through some real battles, to trust in the Sovereign One rather than trying to be a wannabe sovereign myself.

One time I was speaking to a group of young mothers of preschoolers on this very topic, and halfway into my teaching I noticed that the moms were just not following me. Many of them were looking at their phones or even out the window. When I finished speaking, they clapped, but apathetically. I was a little surprised, because this message usually rocks the world of the women in the audience. As I was saying goodbye, an older woman who was a mentor for the group asked to speak with me for a moment. She observed, "Jackie, this group was not listening because they don't think they have an issue with control. They wear their Junior God Badges proudly as competent, responsible, wonderful new mommies."

The lights came on for me. I told her, "When their kids are in elementary school I need to come back and share the same message again." By elementary school—not to mention by middle school and beyond—the Junior God Badge begins to tear a big hole in a young mommy's shirt. At this early stage in their motherhood, they hadn't yet learned that so much is beyond their ability to control.

I'M JUST A GIRL WHO CAN'T SAY *NO*

It may require a considerable amount of time and some rude awakenings for a wannabe sovereign to understand what she's doing. But rude awakenings will come along. A wannabe sovereign gets taken advantage of, because she likes people to think that she can do it all. It's as if she can't say no to anyone's request because that may make her appear uncaring or inadequate. She prides herself on being someone whom everyone else can count on. The more responsible and competent she is, the bigger the flood of requests she will receive. She will be popular! Wannabe sovereign women are on everyone's speed dial list. You've heard the piece of advice: "If you want something done, ask a busy woman." That line is music to her ears. However, I am not sure which is more sad, the fact that she will accept any request or the fact that people keep asking. When will people lovingly offer to do something and take a thing or two off her to-do list—and would she let them if they did?

Recently I overheard my husband mention mildly to one of our friends, "Jackie doesn't have as many speaking engagements scheduled this year." Now, I had two internal responses to that. The healthy part of me squealed "Yahoo! Time to breathe and rest a little." But the old-me response burst right out of my mouth defensively. I defended my schedule by stating that although it was true I wouldn't be doing as many conferences or retreats during the year, I had already written two books and filmed two hundred minutes of a DVD Bible study series. Then I noticed that I must have slipped on my Junior God Badge earlier in the day. (Most days I gladly leave the Junior God Badge in my jewelry box, but other days apparently I can't resist pinning it to my shirt.)

My popularity as a junior sovereign used to bring me so much joy. Then one day a very close friend gently told me the real story. She helped me to see that one reason I was popular was because I always said "yes." "Jackie, you're someone people can easily use." That was the hardest thing for me to hear. I had been thinking people liked to be around me. Well, yes, they did like me; they liked that I fixed everything and was always willing to sacrifice myself for their needs! My friend's observation helped me learn to live on a new level—a few notches below being God's PA—and I learned to check my yesses at the door of His throne room. I have learned how to yield my habitual availability to my sovereign Father and no longer give it away to everyone who asked.

DRONE WOMAN

A junior sovereign learns early how to keep track of her part of the universe; she becomes Drone Woman! Drone Woman hovers above her corner of the universe taking internal pictures of everything that is going on so she can astutely control whatever has an impact on her loved ones.

For example, if the family is going on a trip out of town, Drone Woman determines how much to pack, what to bring, what not to bring, what everyone must have in their carry-on bags, the necessary snack stash, when to leave the house, and more. The list goes on and on. Now, you may be thinking, "What a blessing this woman is to her family!" Yet the negative flip side of this enviable organizational ability is that she incapacitates the ones she loves. Of course now you may be thinking, "If I left all of the packing details up to my children, they would arrive at our vacation destination, and the only things in their suitcases would be an iPad, lots of snacks, and two pairs of underwear. Well, not necessarily. Our children traveled all over with us for years, and I taught them how to pack for themselves. Of course I encouraged them to make stacks on their beds instead of just throwing things into their suitcases, but both of my kids could pack for a mission trip or family vacation by the time they were in the sixth grade. My mother was always amazed at the "little packers" I had. I knew that they would benefit for the rest of their lives from having the skills required—thinking through the days of the trip and reasoning out what they would need.

Too many wannabe sovereigns do everything for their children, and when a child goes off to college, his or her struggles are more than the academic ones. The young adult didn't bring Mom in a suitcase to be the live-in maid, so he or she is often late for class because of sorting through piles of dirty clothes and fast-food bags in search of a missing textbook. The wannabe sovereign forgets to train her children how to live outside the nest without having a nervous breakdown. This Drone Woman hovers over her children to make sure she has the whole picture under control. "They need to concentrate on their studies," she reasons, "so I will take care of everything else." Too many children are passing in school but flunking life.

For me as a controlling woman it seems easier to trust God with a major crisis than with a simple interruption of my schedule. Whether I am planning on spending a few hours writing or an hour trying to answer emails, if suddenly there's an interruption, I can feel such a ridiculous amount of frustration! The more I have learned about God's sovereignty, the more I have come to grasp that the interruptions are actually on God's agenda for my day, even if they absolutely were not on any of *my* multiple to-do lists. (Yes, I have several lists: personal lists, household lists, and ministry lists.) C.S. Lewis wrote a classic paragraph about these aggravating interruptions:

> The great thing, if one can, is to stop regarding all the unpleasant things as interruptions of one's 'own' or 'real' life. The truth is of course that what one calls the interruption are precisely one's real life—the life God is sending one day by day; what one calls one's 'real life' is a phantom of one's own imagination. This at least is what I see at moments of insight: but it's hard to remember it all the time.[11]

Because of the liberating principles in this book, I have come to see the "aggravating interruptions" as more real than the delusional fantasy I create with my own plans for any day of the week or month. Now, when the interruptions occur, it only takes me a few moments to bounce back from Crankyville. Note well: our sovereign God wants to bless us by delivering us from ourselves!

DELUSIONS OF PERSONAL SOVEREIGNTY

Some books seem to be written just for me, and with a title like *The Control Freak*, well, you can understand why this particular one was. I was reading about how to handle the crazy-makers in our lives, and came across a statement that rocked my soul. I knew I would be sharing it with those I love. The first person I called was our daughter, Jessi. I told her that I had just discovered *why* I have a default setting of anxiety and control. What was this revolutionary quote? Drum roll: "Control is a tranquilizer for the anxious person."[12]

The moment I become anxious, I put on my Junior God Badge and become a Control Freak. The more anxious I am, the more controlling I am! Control is my drug of choice. Yet, God's Word clearly states: "Be anxious for *nothing*" (Phil. 4:6 NKJV, emphasis added), which should guide me to the parallel reality of Who is in control and who isn't.

Jessi pondered what I shared, and later in the day she emailed me the following excerpt from a blog by Paul Tripp:

> Many of your struggles are often the result
> of a collision between your plans and God's.
> Although you knew exactly what you wanted

to accomplish and those things that you were determined to avoid, your life didn't unfold as you planned. In some scenarios, it seems as if life is totally out of your control. But, you must rest in the fact that every situation, circumstance, location, experience, and relationship of your life has been under the wise and careful administration of the Lord Almighty.

He has known from the beginning exactly what He was going to do and exactly why He did it. From His vantage point there are no slip-ups, no oversights, no accidents, no misunderstandings, and no mistakes. Nothing has fallen through the cracks…. Psalm 139: "All the days ordained for me were written in your book before one of them came to be" (Psalm 139:16b)….

There's a direct connection between delusions of personal sovereignty and the crushing disappointments that grip us in life. We forget who we are and begin to believe that our hands are really the hands on the joystick. We work with dedication and perseverance, but we work like little sovereigns, rather than resting in the One who is sovereign. God is sovereign. You and I are not.[13]

Do you hear an echo of the wisdom from C.S. Lewis shared above? Reality trumps the delusion. The fact is that *God is in control*. His intricate plan for our lives is not derailed by "interruptions" or "crushing disappointments."

To have confidence in the Lord's sovereignty and to surrender my feelings of anxiety means that I do not need to reach for my favorite drug, control.

REWARDS FOR OBEDIENCE TO THE SOVEREIGN GOD

When I was in college, I was chosen to be in a drama. As you know, part of the work in any play is not only learning your lines, but listening to the director as well. This particular drama was written and directed by the same man. Unfortunately I found myself arguing with the director from time to time regarding where I was supposed to be on the stage. He would mark positions on stage with masking tape so that we would know where to stand; because *he*, the director, knew where the microphones would be and how the lighting would be set up. Well, I didn't always want to stand where the tape was. For some reason, I thought I knew better. The director would often have to say to me, "Jackie, don't move beyond your piece of tape or you will not be seen by the audience!"

As I have studied the sovereignty of God, I realize that He is both the scriptwriter and the director of my life. It is He who has very specifically placed tape on the stage of my life to keep me within range of the lighting and the microphone. Under the spotlight, I can reflect His glory. Near the microphones, I can declare His goodness to this dark world.

Our whole Christian life is about paying attention to the scriptwriter's direction. God has patiently taught me that He is the sovereign Playwright and blessed Director of the universe. God is also the Stage Manager of my life, He knows exactly where I need to be. He knows right where my toes need to line up with the tape in order for me to remain in the safest place on earth: smack in the center of His will. I am embarrassed to admit that I not only argued with my college theater director, I have also argued with God Almighty, the ultimate playwright and director. Foolishly, I have tried to reposition the masking tape on the stage of my life. As a wannabe sovereign, I have often thought I knew a position that would suit me better. Do you know what I'm talking about here? Have you sometimes argued with the sovereign Director, too?

Centuries ago, the minister and theologian John Calvin taught a profound truth about the seriousness of understanding God's sovereignty. I will boil it down to a simple declarative statement: The Christian who does not understand God's sovereignty will be miserable, but the Christian who does understand God's sovereignty will be blessed. I have observed this to be 100 percent true, and have found that nothing displays our understanding of His sovereignty more clearly than a crisis. The unfolding of a crisis exposes both the misery and the blessedness.

The nature of a crisis reveals the content of the life of the person who is facing the crisis. In other words, a crisis reveals the stuff we are made of. It unveils our true character, and God can use this to loosen our grip on the gifts He has given us in life. Some of us hang on to what we've been given with an iron grip. We panic at the prospect of God taking this person or that thing out of our lives. Of course the panic only proves that we have made an idol of this particular object or person.

In Genesis 22, we read how God asked Abraham to offer Isaac as a living sacrifice. This was a significant request, because Abraham knew that the heathen worshippers of Molech sacrificed their firstborn sons. But God was doing a deep work in Abraham that required great surrender and unquestioned trust. At that moment when he lifted the knife to slay his only son, Abraham was foreshadowing what God would do to Jesus on the cross, and he was also displaying his own unwavering surrender to God. God was cleansing him of what can be referred to as an "uncleansed love"—loving his "late life" child a little too much.

Do you have an uncleansed love in your life right now, a love that is in competition with loving God supremely? Do you panic at the mere thought of losing something or someone? I had to reassess the state of my heart when two good friends were widowed within forty-two days of each other. My husband and I were about to celebrate forty years of marriage, and both of us got tears in our eyes at the thought of life here on earth without each other. I don't know how many times I have given this fear to God, genuinely seeking to cherish each day together and to avoid anxiety or panic.

God sometimes needs helps us let go of things that are just too important to us. I have come to call this "pre-exit stripping." Remember Job's initial response to his prolonged crisis? "Naked I came from my mother's womb, and naked I will depart" (Job 1:21). We will all leave this earth "naked." Even if we should die fully clothed, we will be as bared open to God as the day we were born, taking nothing with us, just as we brought nothing with us. Well, I have found that the Lord does some of this "stripping" long before we actually exit this life, and that's what why I call it "pre-exit stripping."

God used this verse years ago to comfort me when something very precious to me was lost. We were at one of my son's games cheering enthusiastically, because our team was doing exceptionally well against a very tough opponent. We were also jumping up and down to keep warm on a cool night. As I went to remove my sweatshirt shortly after arriving home, I suddenly noticed that I was no longer wearing my diamond necklace. This was a very special necklace. It had been made by my father and it had my name, *Jackie*, written in diamonds. The diamonds had all come from my mother's wedding ring set. It was irreplaceable. To say that I was in a slight panic would be an understatement.

My husband and son immediately decided they were going back to the stadium in the dark with flashlights to search under the stands where we had been cheering so crazily. As he rushed out the door, my precious husband tried to reassure me, "We're going to find it; don't worry."

But all I could say was, "Sweetheart, it's gone." As they drove away I knew in my heart that they would not find the necklace.

Hours later when Ken and Ben returned—without my necklace, I told Ken that I had known they wouldn't find it. He tried to comfort me with the promise of another necklace, but I told him it was simply not replaceable. The next morning, during my quiet time with Jesus, He gave me this passage from Job and whispered, "Trust Me with this pre-exit stripping." The Spirit of God allowed me to wear black for a week to mourn this pre-exit stripping.

Now every time I see a picture from the past with me wearing the necklace—I had worn it literally every day for twelve years—I am reminded again about letting go and being at peace with pre-exit stripping. I hear the Lord whisper to my soul, "I want you to practice letting go. Don't hang onto things too tightly, Jackie. They are gifts. They are to be appreciated for a moment, but not worshipped." I know there are far worse losses that will take more than a week of grieving to mourn—but I also know that even in those losses, one can still trust God's sovereignty. Nancy Guthrie wrote the following after burying her second child:

> When you come to the place where you recognize that everything you have and everyone you love is a gift, it becomes possible to enjoy those gifts, not with an attitude of greed, but one of gratitude. You and I, like Job, know that God gives and God takes away, and when He takes away, if we are able to focus on the joy of what was given, if only for a short time, we take another step toward the pathway to the heart of God.[14]

SOVEREIGNTY: UNLIKELY ROUTE TO JOY

Whenever I read about deportation (a person or persons being expelled from their homes or country), I never consider it to be a good thing. Recently I was reading about the deportation of two particular Jews, Aquila and Priscilla. Claudius Caesar had first ruled that the Jews would not be allowed to have meetings, and then he decided to expel them from Rome. Having been deported from their home and country, Aquila and Priscilla ended up in Corinth. Little did these two tentmakers know that their expulsion would become an unlikely route to joy. In Corinth, they not only had Paul the apostle working with them as a part-time tentmaker, they were also invited to be part of his traveling Gospel team:

> Then Paul left Athens and went to Corinth. There he became acquainted with a Jew named Aquila, born in Pontus, who had recently arrived from Italy with his wife, Priscilla. They had left Italy when Claudius Caesar deported all Jews from Rome. Paul lived and worked with them, for they were tentmakers just as he was (Acts 18:1-3, NLT).

Oh, if only we as God's kids would have the attitude that our "deportations" from what we love, hometown, job, church, or friends, are really chances for us to see God's brilliant maneuvering into a place where He will receive even more glory through our lives. Rather than resisting change or resenting the upheaval of your life, why not look forward to seeing who or what God may bring into your life-walk after your expulsion from your comfort zone. When Aquila and Priscilla were packing up their earthly possessions because of a cruel expulsion edict, they could have had no idea, apart from their trust in God's faithfulness, what lay ahead during their forced relocation. Aquila and Priscilla's deportation reminds us again to keep whatever comes into our lives in the context of God's ever-present capacity to take what is intended for evil and bring about good (see Genesis 50:20).

Actively trusting God when we get deported from comfort and security gives us a chance to make our canyon of pain into a megaphone as we proclaim the ultimate goodness and sovereignty of God. In his book, *31 Days Toward Trusting God*, Jerry Bridges writes:

> God does whatever pleases Him. This is the essence of God's sovereignty; His absolute independence to do as He pleases and His absolute control over the actions of all His creatures. No creature, person, or empire can either thwart His will or act outside the bounds of it.[15]

You may feel that this sounds "unfair" or "unloving." Maybe the phrase, "He does as He pleases" terrifies you, especially considering the stack of blueprints that you have already drawn up for your life and lives of those you love. This quote represents an enormous challenge for the wannabe sovereign woman; she finds it so hard to trust in God's absolute control. The difference between a woman who fares terribly during a bad time of suffering and a woman who does amazingly well is the latter's understanding that our sovereign God is also our loving Father God, and His love for His children serves as a filter for all suffering. We need to remember that He did not spare His only Son as a demonstration of the redemptive quality of suffering and that even Jesus, "although He was a son, He learned obedience through the things He suffered" (Heb. 5:8, NET).

So what builds confidence in God's sovereignty? This hope is developed by intentional clinging to God and His Word. When a woman spends time in God's Word, she tightens her hold on God's hand, almost as if her developing faith "tapes" her hand to God's. Now whenever she trips, she will not fall face-down, because God's hand steadies her as she regains her balance. When she rises daily to spend time reading the Word, it is like applying fresh tape to that hand. With her grip reinforced, she is ready to accept the good, the bad, and even the ugly by faith! As the Word puts it, "faith comes by hearing, and hearing by the Word of God" (Rom. 10:17, NKJV).

In contrast, the wannabe sovereign does not have her hand taped to the Lord's. Instead of spending hours in prayer and the Word, she spends hours trying to keep a firm grip on those she loves to keep them from stubbing their toes! The wannabe sovereign woman does not have time to strengthen her grip on God's hand by spending time in His Word: She is too busy stuffing her hand into God's suggestion box with all her prayerful ideas on how to protect the people she loves. If she were in the Word, she would know that Jesus already prayed before leaving earth for those He loved—both then and in the future—to be protected:

> I will remain in the world no longer but they are still in the world, and I am coming to You. Holy Father, **protect** them by the power of Your name, the name You gave Me…. While I was with them, I **protected** them and kept them safe by that name You gave Me (John 17:11-12, emphasis added).

In the final analysis, God's protection and safety and provision will always outweigh the hazards. At a women's conference years ago, one of the speakers asked the audience to get out a blank sheet of paper. On one side we were to write the word *GOOD*, and on the back side we were to write the word *BAD*. Then we were instructed to start writing the good things we have received from the Lord and a list of the bad things the Lord has permitted to come into our lives. The speaker said that she anticipated that our *GOOD* list would exceed our *BAD* list. For me, it was so true, and those around me had the same experience. On top of that, God can take even the desolate areas on our *BAD* list and transform them into a place of delight: "No longer will they call you Deserted, or name your land Desolate. But you will be called Hephzibah (My delight is in her), and your land Beulah" (Isa. 62:4).

Time and time again, sitting securely in the center of God's sovereignty, I have watched God transform my desperate and discouraging situation into something delightful. I can almost hear God whispering a new nick-name for me—*Heppy* (for Hephzibah, "My delight is in her").

I am not the only one who is making this discovery. A woman named Jenell Bianchini posted the following on Facebook several years ago:

> For me, control was a subtle necessity that I believe satan wove into my consciousness at a young age. I looked around at age four or five and realized there was no one to really take care of me. It was then I began to believe that I was the God of my universe, and everything that happened from then on became my responsibility.
>
> So when things were good, I took the credit; and when things went south, I struggled with that weight. Fear drove this need to see into the future so that I could head things off at the pass before I got hurt. I lived on "lookout mountain" for a very long time—until I found Jesus! When I finally began to trust *Him* with it *all* (a process still ongoing), I understood the passage "Come to me all who are weary and I will give you rest." We are not meant to carry all this weight. When I shifted mine to the Lord, I was free at last!
>
> I live each day measuring myself up to God's standards, and I now can truly answer the question in the Bible "Are you here to please man, or are you here to please God" with the only answer for a Princess, a daughter of the King: I am here

to please you, Father! You are my God, my Lord, and my Savior.

FROM GROANING TO GLORY BY FAITH

I have *groaned* more in the past twelve months than I have in years. I have listened to so many painful situations in the lives of the people I love that my groaning has sometimes felt suffocating. One time in the middle of such deep groaning, I cried out to the Lord for a fresh word on bringing God's glory in the midst of groaning. The answer began with a passage in Romans 8:18-26, where I found the word "groaning" used. I could see three different "groaners": Creation (v. 22), Christians (v. 23), and the Holy Spirit (v. 26). Now, I was not surprised about Creation groaning, because I knew it was like birth pangs. Nor was I surprised by Christians groaning; unfortunately, I hear that choir of groans regularly. What grabbed my heart was that the Holy Spirit, the Paraclete, the Comforter, is a "Co-Groaner" with us.

Consider this: Whenever you groan or sigh, the Co-Groaner is ready to intercede on your behalf. Let this passage soak into your sighing soul right now: "In the same way, the Spirit helps us in our weakness, for we do not know how we should pray, but the Spirit Himself intercedes for us with inexpressible groanings" (Rom. 8:26, NET).

We all groan at one time or another, on our own behalf and for the sake of those we love. Our groaning can be complaining and despairing, or it can be a chance to bring glory to God by trusting Him with that which is unreasonable, unfathomable, unfair, disproportionate, relentless, and so forth. With every new chance to "groan," I find myself smiling when I remember my Co-Groaner, and I find that it's easier to bring God glory by choosing to trust Him with the outcome!

The wannabe sovereign groans about what she cannot control, and "surrender" is not part of her vocabulary. To surrender appears to her like quitting. She hasn't learned how to trust the Lord who co-groans with her.

THE GLORY OF BEING EPHRAIM

Suffering pulls the lid off your life and lets the glory of Jesus shine out. Out of something painful, something beautiful can grow. Let's look at pulling the lid off of one's life to release the glory. Here is one of my favorite examples: the glory of Ephraim (see Genesis 41:50-52).

While Joseph was in Egypt, he had two sons. He named the first one Manasseh, and he named the second one Ephraim. Manasseh means "God has helped me to forget the troubles in my father's household." The lid has begun to be lifted, but it is not totally open until we learn the name of Joseph's second-born son, Ephraim. Ephraim means "God has made me fruitful in a place of suffering." *Now* the lid is totally lifted, and the glory has a chance to be released. Why do I say this?

There are two methods for handling suffering. There are some people who just survive it, get through it, and forget it—that would be Manasseh. Other people come through suffering, and they become fruitful; gardens are planted in the center of their pain—that would be Ephraim. People are encouraged by this person's courage to hang on to Jesus. Some people are survivors, while others are more than survivors, *they are fruitful in suffering.* They have learned to not waste their suffering.

A mom who had a child killed by a drunk driver starts a movement to encourage other parents who have been through similar tragedy—that's fruitful in suffering. People who lose a loved one and they not only attend Grief Share, but they encourage others to come and be encouraged—that is an Ephraim lifestyle. People who go through painful divorce can either just survive and join a sorority of bitter divorcees, or the divorced person can go to Divorce Recovery and not only heal but begin to help others heal—that is Ephraim.

In 1990, my younger sister killed herself. On the flight home for the funeral, I was musing about a painful past that my sister could not forget. Then, six months later, my dad suddenly died. He was not a follower of Jesus, and the reality of his dying without the hope of being forever with God caused a Grand-Canyon-sized pain in my soul. God taught me, "Jackie, I want you to be more than a survivor. I want you to be fruitful in a place of suffering." This was the beginning of the Glory of Ephraim in my life.

As soon as suffering enters your life, a platform comes with it, and you have to decide what you're going to do on the platform. Are you going to let God pull the lid off your life and reveal His Glory? Are you going to tape your hand to God's and hang on to hope, believing that He's good, no matter what? Are you going to give hope to other people, too? Or, are you just going to get through it somehow, and merely survive? There are a lot of survivors who don't bless people, and they are often very cranky people. When you suffer, are you more like Manasseh or Ephraim?

The choice is yours, and you know what God wants you to do.

DISCUSSION QUESTIONS

1. Discuss: The wannabe sovereign actually sees herself as an honorary personal assistant to God. (See Colossians 1:17.)

2. Are you aggravated by interruptions? What kind and when? Is your life more a picture of resting in His control, or of a quest for your own control? (See Psalm 46:10.)

3. Spend a few moments discussing what the following quote means to you. "The Christian who does not understand God's sovereignty will be miserable, but the Christian who understands God's sovereignty will be blessed." (See Psalm 16:5; 115:1-3.)

4. Consider this quote: "Control is a tranquilizer for the anxious person." Are you happiest when you are sovereignly in control of your world? Why? (See 1 Thessalonians 5:24; Deuteronomy 2:7.)

5. The following verses remind us that God is sovereign and we are not, and that believing this gives you a most blessed place to rest. Consider memorizing one or more of them:
    *   Psalm 139:16
    *   2 Timothy 1:9
    *   Isaiah 25:1; 43:7,10-11

- Ephesians 1:4-5,11; 2:10

6. Discuss for a moment the principle of going from "groaning to glory" with the help of the "Co-Groaner." (See Romans 8:18-26.)

7. Share a personal illustration of the Glory of Ephraim in your life. (See Genesis 41:52)

CHAPTER 8

CHRONIC FATIGUE OF CONTROL

You have now been introduced to the wannabe-omnipres-ent-omnipotent-omniscient-Jehovah-Shalom-sovereign-con-trolled-by-fear, *proud owner* of an entire collection of Junior God Badges…. are you exhausted yet? I am, just from writing that! The big lie of the drive to control is that it empowers us. On the contrary, here's the truth: Controlling causes great fatigue. Not just some fatigue sometimes, but *chronic fatigue.*

The chronic fatigue of control is not something that most women want to acknowledge—whether young or old, but we are going to examine this tired woman. The people in the balcony of her life already *know* she is tired, but she may not know it—yet!

Recently a mature woman disclosed to a small group of friends that whenever she would hear references to control, she assumed it was not her issue. Now, bone-tired and with little reserve energy, she was able to admit that all her "holy sweat" to heal her child's marriage was actually fueled by control. She confessed the audacity on her part that caused her to think she could change or control the intentions of another human being. She had trespassed into God's territory, because He is the *only one* who can change a human being.

Let's look at what a lifetime of control produces in the Junior God Badge owner. We will examine some results the wannabe deity can look forward to with the acronym T-I-R-E-D.

T: TRAPPED

The controlling woman often feels trapped, because she consistently says "Yes" when she should have said "No." Ironically, what she hopes to accomplish before lunch time is not only delusional, it's what she does in her desperate attempt to *not* feel so trapped. The controlling woman assumes that if she runs faster today than any previous day, she will finally get a break and some necessary rest. No sooner does she notice a break in her schedule than something happens to fill the empty slot.

Our lives are more than a dream in God's heart, and a woman who is constantly striving to control everything in the lives of those she loves will often miss the script written for her own life even before Genesis 1:1. Yes, the Word of God states that God's script for your life and mine existed *before* Creation:

Who hath saved us, and called us with a holy calling, not according to our works, but according to His own purpose and grace, which was given to us in Christ Jesus before the world began (2 Tim. 1:9, KJV, emphasis added).

I have spent years grieving the amount of time I have wasted, running around, trying to control my little universe—all the while running past the very script and purpose of my life. I was too often so busy trying to micromanage the lives of others that I missed doing the very things that God saved me to do. When a woman is chronically fatigued by her controlling pace, she can't even discern between God's script and the whining demands of her dysfunctional family. But look at this extraordinary fact that Scripture tells us about God's script for our lives. Pause this moment and read—and then reread—this well-known verse: "For we are God's handiwork [masterpiece], created in Christ Jesus to do good works, which *God prepared in advance for us to do*" (Eph. 2:10, emphasis added).

Did you catch the emphasis? God prepared *in advance* what He wants from us. He wants it from us, because it's part of His blueprint for each particular "masterpiece" He has created. The tragedy is that a "trapped" lifestyle blurs this heavenly masterpiece. In fact, sometimes our insistence to run our own lives is like spray-painting graffiti all over that masterpiece of a life.

A very exhausted young mom wrote me an email two weeks before Christmas, describing how trapped she was feeling. Her honesty is refreshing and such a clear reminder of the chronic fatigue of the young as well as old when trying to control an untamable universe:

> These last few weeks have worn me out. I'm exhausted, and I just need a break from Christmas. With four kids, two businesses, and the Christmas clock ticking, I continually feel behind. I'm late almost everywhere. I've missed appointments, missed my kids, and sometimes—even missed my sanity. It's like this every Christmas for us, as it probably is for you, too, but this year has been especially hard.
>
> Sometimes I just a need a "time out," but I feel trapped. Trapped by school programs, a vicious work schedule, and, sometimes, even church demands. Christmas cards to be addressed, presents to be wrapped, meals to be planned, a house to be cleaned, and there are friends I haven't talked to in weeks. This list of failures and the random tears are the evidence that perhaps I'm not balancing this right. My schedule is filled with good things—great things even—but in this rushed pace, I am missing something, and I think it's making me crazy.
>
> The reality is, I often continue this craziness and exhaustion until I am worn ragged. *I dish out fractions of myself everywhere, but I'm not wholeheartedly invested anywhere.* Have you ever been there?

Are you too trapped to do the good works the Lord has prepared for you to do? Can you think of a time this past week when you did something that you felt trapped to do and you didn't feel the liberty to do what you knew deep in your heart Papa God wanted you to do? Are you ready to remove your Junior God Badge and be more freed up to do the good works God planned for you? Maybe you are not ready yet to surrender your script for His, because the many demands of those around you is louder than that holy nudge within. Well, that mindset can lead us right into the next letter of TIRED—*I*.

I: IRRITATED

The controlling woman is not only trapped, she is irritated by an ever-expanding to-do list. She is convinced that after she writes out her list at night for the next day someone comes in and adds to it while she is sleeping! This woman is irritated by everything she "has" to do *and* all those things that daily upset her arranged life. She feels that she is constantly getting all her ducks in a row, only to have some mysterious visitor come by and knock some of those ducks out of line!

In 2007 I saw an advertisement in *Forbes Magazine* that included a working woman's to-do list. I tore it out and it has been in a file folder since then. On the page I wrote, "the exhausted HCIC." Here is the list from her Day-Timer (the lists we now keep on our smart phones):

- Wake-up (coffee to go)

- Last-minute packing

- Call cab (hope it comes)

- Check in

- Hour in security (remember to take out laptop)

- Flight (middle seat)

- Sit uncomfortably as passenger falls asleep on shoulder

- Sit on landing strip for hours

- Rush to meeting

- Present for half hour

- Flight home (eat before flight)

- Lose feeling in legs

- Taxi home (bring enough cash)

- Call therapist

- Unpack

- Cry self to sleep

This list may seem kind of silly to you, but this is the type of list that actually scrolls through the soul of every woman—unless she's in a coma. Women wake up every day to an inevitable to-do list! Even the most laid-back woman still has things she plans to do. She may procrastinate before getting to the first item on her list—but she has a list. Now, this irritation is not just a modern issue. Women not being able to control their universe has been a conundrum from the earliest times of mankind. I think of the controlling Israelite woman when I look at this ancient passage:

> *Whenever the cloud lifted from above the tent, the Israelites set out; whenever the cloud settled, the Israelites encamped. At the Lord's command the Israelites set out, and at His command they encamped. As long as the cloud stayed over the tabernacle, they remained in camp. When the cloud remained over the tabernacle* **a long time***, the Israelites obeyed the Lord's order and did not set out. Sometimes the cloud was over the tabernacle* **only a few days***; at the Lord's command they would encamp, and then at His command they would set out. Sometimes the cloud stayed* **only from evening till morning***, and when it lifted in the morning, they set out.* **Whether by day or by night***, whenever the cloud lifted, they set out. Whether the cloud stayed over the tabernacle for* **two days, or a month or a year***, the Israelites would remain in camp and not set out; but when it lifted, they would set out* (Num. 9:17-22, emphasis added).

Whenever I have read this passage, I can totally see myself setting up my tent and then suddenly hearing a trumpet sound that meant the cloud was moving, hence we were moving. I could actually feel the irritation of a woman finally getting her tent settled and then hearing the trumpet and ignoring its blast—convinced that *surely* the cloud couldn't be moving already. I could hear the internal self-talk of the irritated controller who wants to refuse to pack up what she has just unpacked. I can image that I would have battled with unpacking in the first place, given the unpredictable probability that I might be re-packing in the morning—or even in the middle of the night.

The applications to this situation the Israelites faced are many, but I will tell you about a group of women I have known for years who experience a pretty literal version of such uncertainty in their lives: baseball wives. During spring training, their husbands routinely find out that they are not going back to the team they loved, but are moving to another team in a city that is nowhere near their home or the place they rented the previous baseball season. Also, there are times during the baseball season when, after a game, the manager calls in a player and tells him that he is being sent down to a minor league team. He gets no warning, just "bye-bye"! And his wife? The wife has finally set up her tent in a strange city, and then she hears a "trumpet" when her husband comes home and tells her that they are moving again—*today!* No warning, no consideration, no concern about the price to the wife and family—talk about an irritation! Although all baseball wives have been warned that is part of the game, they are never ready for the sound of the trumpet and the surprise move after just feeling settled. I know one baseball player's wife who went through two seasons of this unpredictable moving. She moved ten times in only two seasons.

So, the next time you feel *trapped* and *irritated* by the demands and unpredictability of life, remember, you are in good company. Pray for someone who may be in an even more dramatic situation than you are, and *believe* that the Lord has a plan to work in and through you—His script for your life. In that process of walking through your script, you have a choice about how you respond to things, which brings us to the *R* of TIRED.

R: RIGID VS. FLEXIBLE

At a conference in Orlando, speaker Dan Allender made a statement that captured a truth: "The mature Christian is one who understands that life is more chaotic than predictable!" When he made this remark, some people laughed, but most of the audience groaned. Let's admit it, chaos is a controller's nightmare. In response to chaos, however, the incomparable Oswald Chambers describes "gracious uncertainty" as a mark of spiritual maturity:

> Certainty is the mark of the common-sense life; gracious uncertainty is the mark of the spiritual life. To be certain of God means that we are uncertain in all our ways, we do not know what a day may bring forth we are uncertain of the next step, but we are certain of God.... He packs our life with surprises all the time.[16]

How brilliant is this! Yet how challenging! To "not know what a day may bring forth" is terrifying for the controlling woman. Generally speaking, controlling women hate surprises (unless they are planning them). Chambers is describing gripping onto God and letting go of everything else. How willing are you to grow in this area of spiritual maturity?

I was talking with my best friend, DeDe, recently, and she said, "I know we have always referred to life being more chaotic than predictable. But now I think you and I have lived long enough to really *believe* that chaos in the lives of those we love has become predictable." We both laughed, but I couldn't wait to include her remark in this chapter. The rigid controlling woman has not come to terms with this reality. This rigid woman will know she has come to terms with the predictability of chaos when having her ducks knocked out of their neat row will not knock her for a loop.

Oh the glorious "gracious uncertainty" that each day brings! It's a new chance to turn our hearts toward God, surrender our irritation and ask the Holy Spirit to take away our rigidity. These are God's tutorials in flexibility— He's stretching us! Now every time in the airport I see the posting of a delay for my flight, I am able to smile and keep reading the book I have with me, knowing that the delay is a reminder of the predictability of chaos with air travel. The accident on the highway that slows traffic to an absolute standstill is another reminder of the predictability of chaos, and an opportunity to pray for the people in the accident or other motorists around you. Maybe that's *exactly* the work God prepared for you in advance for that hour. A terminal diagnosis of cancer is also predictable chaos in this world outside the Garden, and along with its grief, it includes countless opportunities for the glory of God to shine. What can we control? We can only control our *attitude* about the predictable chaos.

Another *R* aspect of the TIRED, controlling woman is Resentful; R stands for that, too.

One morning I watched a group of women on the *Today Show* who were discussing their frustration with being called a nag or a shrew when they felt all they were trying to do was control the chaos and bring order to their family or workplace. These women were clearly resentful that their families expected them to "do it all" without ever giving in to the urge to nag. They resented the fact that in the workplace, a man who controls and directs is seen as a leader, whereas a woman who tries to control and direct is seen as a nagging shrew.

I actually understand their complaints. Throughout my life I have heard sarcastic remarks about my need to lead or how controlling I must have to be in order to get everything done. Some men have seen me as overbearing and they wished I would just zip shut my "pie hole"! Men in the church have assumed I was controlling simply because I was loud. These men did not realize that my husband exhibits awesome strength and that he is totally the one leading in our home—no matter how loud I get.

I will admit to being a nag as I glance through all the things I need to get done and start barking out quick orders to everyone who is sitting on the couch watching another movie or sports event (okay…except for the playoffs!). When my husband first started to work with me in managing my ministry, Power to Grow, I would run through a list of all the things we needed to get done by the next conference, and he would just stare at me and not say much. One day I walked into his office and he was sitting in a chair… just staring. I asked him if he was okay, and his reply was not totally surprising to me. He kindly said, "I don't know if I can work with you!" I actually burst out laughing at first, and then I sat down and asked him to explain why working with me seemed like an un-scalable mountain. His calm reply was, "When you come into the office and start rattling off a list of all the things we need to get done, it is like a machine gun was just fired, and I am lost after the first three things on your list." Ken and I have now worked together for nine years, because I put away my machine gun and switched to writing out what needs to be done. I no longer dictate; instead I jot down what needs to be accomplished. I even include on the memo what I would like to have so that I can feel good about an upcoming event— such as booking a flight that arrives early enough. (I would always like to settle into the ministry event rather than breathlessly bursting through the conference door just in time to speak to the waiting audience.)

Do you know what this simple change in my style of communication and organizing has accomplished? It has brought the "resentful factor" way down—for both Ken and me! I no longer feel like a shrew or resent "having" to be a nag. And my dear husband doesn't resent me for my overbearing tendencies.

One of the most common control techniques employed by women is nagging. Naturally, women resent references to nagging about as much as they hate jokes about PMS. I once led a Bible study that focused on the topic, "When a Man Doesn't Need a Woman." We talked about a woman's tendency to want to control her children as well as her husband. One day I mustered enough courage to read some of the common biblical references about nagging women. It is interesting to note that in the same proverb a foolish child and a quarrelsome wife are seen as painful. Too often when a woman does not stop nagging, a quarrel is inevitable. For example:

> *Better to live on a corner of the roof than share a house with a quarrelsome wife* (Prov. 21:9).

> *Better to live in a desert than with a quarrelsome and nagging wife* (Prov. 21:19).

> *A quarrelsome wife is like the dripping of a leaky roof in a rainstorm; restraining her is like restraining the wind or grasping oil with the hand* (Prov. 27:15-16).

> *A foolish child is a father's ruin, and a quarrelsome wife is like the constant dripping of a leaky roof* (Prov. 19:13).

We see in Proverbs 21:9 that a man is better off being a "rooftop-dweller" than he is if he lives in a house with a nagging woman. As I finished reading that verse, in my imagination I saw a man placing a ladder on the side of his house and hurrying up the ladder to his roof. I started laughing at the thought of a man having to sit on his roof to escape his nagging wife and find a moment of peace (with the God who made his wife)!

As I thought about the concept of a man having a place to hurry away to when his wife begins to nag, I brainstormed a trip to Home Depot where a woman could buy a ladder and place it on the side of her house with a ribbon around it for Father's Day. Then, the next time Mommy starts nagging Daddy, he can calmly walk out the door, climb the ladder, and wait for her to calm down. Have you ever seen those ladders that have some "give" to them? They are sturdy but can bend a little when someone hurries up them. I envisioned a whole neighborhood where men were sitting on their rooftops just after dinner. Just think of all the fights that this ladder could prevent. What a quiet but potent visual reminder that nagging never changed one individual on planet Earth!

As I thought about the escape ladder, the Lord showed me that most men already have their escape routes figured out, whether it means tinkering in the garage, hunting every weekend (see Proverbs 21:19), staring at the TV or computer, or even sitting behind the newspaper. Each man develops his own technique of muting his wife's voice. The saddest aspect of this reality is when a man must develop a means of muting his wife's nagging voice, he also inadvertently mutes her voice of love, encouragement, wisdom, and respect.

If you look more closely at the words "nagging" and "quarrelsome," you will discover that these words come from a Hebrew word that means "contentious" and "contest." Too often my nagging flows from the contest between my script and my family's agenda. How about you?

Are you seeing more reasons to remove your Junior God Badge? Are you ready to become a reformed nag? If not, here is some more motivation to retire from being a TIRED, controlling woman.

E: EXHAUSTED

Consider how we can grab the burden of tomorrow even in our dreams. When the controlling woman finally falls asleep, she has many dreams of being in total panic, knowing she can't possibly get everything done. This woman lives with the serious stresses and strains of an out-of-control world. Being exhausted is not a new experience for most of the daughters of Eve, but the twenty-first century seems to have doubled if not tripled the exhaustion in the life of all Evettes.

Why do intelligent women ignore the red indicator light on their lives? I can look at a friend's life and see that she is doing cartwheels on the edge of a steep cliff with her breathless pace, but she has no clue about the danger of her proximity to the edge. Why does a woman have to become really sick to even slow down for a moment? Even when she has pneumonia she is still doing four loads of clothes, making dinner for her family, answering hundreds of emails and clearing a path through the family room that looks like a disaster scene. Oh, this woman has taken her medicine, but she simply won't rest enough for the virus to dissipate. Do you know this woman? Is she a friend? Is she a relative? Is this you I am writing about?

When I read the following quote, two sentences clarify why women ignore the red indicator light on their lives.

> Many people commit to a 120% life and wonder why the burden feels so heavy. It is rare to see a life pre-schedule to only 80%, leaving a margin for responding to the unexpected God sends our way. [17]

Let's look a little closer at these two sentences. Consider the last few days of your life. Were your days based on a "120% life" schedule? I have friends who believe that you are not giving God your best unless you are committed to living life at 120% (or more). Whenever I communicate with those friends, they are constantly rehearsing all that they are doing on a daily, monthly, and yearly basis. I actually get exhausted just listening to the litany. I used to think that God is most pleased with the members of this 120% Club! Then I realized that this club was not impressing God in the least. Sure, they may impress other people, but this lifestyle also massages the pride of the club members.

Now the second sentence holds the key to a life that God can freely interrupt and bless with the most divine of appointments. Committing yourself to an 80% schedule is a faith choice that gives God the liberty to use you as He pleases. Too many people have to have a car accident for God to get their attention and send the divine appointments that He designed for their life.

A dear friend of mine regularly reminds me of the fuel of pride that motivates the 120% life schedule, as opposed to the humble, faith-filled 80% life schedule. When you see space in your schedule, don't immediately cram it full of people-pleasing appointments. Leave that space open and cheerfully anticipate that Papa God may have a surprise for you. Remember, it is impossible to please God without faith (Heb. 11:6), and for a controlling woman it is a major work of faith to commit to an 80% schedule rather than the impressive, breathless, 120% life schedule.

From time to time, I read from an awesome devotional, *A Minute of Margin* that addresses the need for balance and healthy "margin" in our lives. The book is packed full of classic comments, but the following one really spoke to me. The book was written by a physician, Dr. Richard A Swenson, and this quote is from a fellow doctor named Dr. James M. Cerletty:

> I am dying of easy accessibility. Telephones in our homes and offices, cordless phones in our backyards and cars, beepers, fax machines, and e-mail. It's enough to give you a stroke. If Alexander Graham Bell walked into my office, I'd

punch him in the nose. If he called, you can be sure I'd put him on hold.[18]

And do you know what? Dr. Cerletty said this before we had cell phones, texting, Twitter, Facebook, and Instagram, along with their accessibility overload and CPA (chronic partial attention)!

On New Year's Day, I was in an ICU speaking with a nurse about the irreparable damage done by a massive stroke my mom's second husband had suffered (he died six days later). While the ICU nurse was trying to delicately explain the painful situation to my mom, my husband and me, my phone was vibrating with multiple texts! It was New Year's Day and people were sending me their best wishes. Of course no one knew I was in an ICU. While scrolling through many texts on the drive home from the hospital, I was again reminded of the 24/7 accessibility overload that bombards all our lives. One of the texts was somebody inquiring if I were on Instagram. In that moment, to be honest, I just about cussed!

I've heard it said that how a person makes you feel when you are with her is a mirror of how she feels inside. What the exhausted woman cannot see is that she is exhausting to be around. Her drained life is a drain on others. So, when I am exhausted and drained and cranky, I am not a gift to anyone around me. And isn't that ironic, considering the fact that I *think* everything I am doing is for everyone else! "A cheerful disposition is good for your health; gloom and doom leave you bone-tired" (Prov. 17:22, MSG). My exhaustion and crankiness produces gloom and doom not only for me but also for anyone who has to be around me! Haven't you spent time with a person and ended up with a bad headache? I know my hyper pace has worn out friends who have spent a day with me.

The principle of the exhausted one exhausting others was actually addressed in the book of Exodus during a conversation between Moses and his father-in-law Jethro. While Jethro was visiting Moses, he watched as people came to Moses from morning until evening. Throngs of people were standing all around Moses as he judged and gave God's counsel. Rather than being impressed with all that Moses did all day, Jethro expressed his concern:

> *What you are doing is not good. You and these people who come to you will only wear yourselves out. The work is too heavy for you; you cannot handle it alone* (Exod. 18:17-18).

> *Thou wilt surely wear away, both thou, and this people that is with thee* (Exod. 18:18, KJV).

Now, you may be thinking about your family lounging around, watching TV, and you can't see how they are being worn out by their overworked mama. Well, surely they are affected by your less-than-delightful disposition at the dinner table! They are getting worn out by your irritable, rigid, resentful responses to them because you're so *exhausted*. In addition, the people you work with are impacted by your exhaustion—not only in the mistakes you might make, but also the remarks that flow from your mouth—your whining and complaining. We will discuss this "native tongue" of the controller at the end of this chapter.

But finally, one more aspect of the controlling, TIRED woman. She is D-for-Defensive.

D: DEFENSIVE

Defensiveness displays itself in many ways in the life of a Junior God woman. We get defensive when we have to explain our elaborate desires for things to be done our way on our time schedule. We feel defensive when we resent how someone else has characterized us. Interestingly, defensiveness is revealed by the things we do and by the things we don't do. In the tribe of Omni-Super Women, we can act as each other's worst enemies. The controlling woman is constantly having to explain why she can't get it all done! It is almost like she walks into a courtroom every day to be evaluated and judged by a jury of her peers. She drives to events rehearsing what she will say to a particular "prosecuting" woman who won't even say hello without immediately questioning her about what she's doing, what she has gotten done, when she's going to get it done....

Recently I was reading an article called "7 Habits of Chronically Unhappy People," and point number 5 just jumped out of my computer screen. This is something the defensive woman needs to consider, especially when approached by a prosecuting friend.

> #5. You strive to control your life. There's a difference between control and striving to achieve our goals. Happy people take steps daily to achieve their goals, but realize in the

end, there's very little control over what life throws their way. Unhappy people tend to micromanage in an effort to control all outcomes and then fall apart in dramatic display when life throws a wrench in their plan. Happy people can be just as focused, yet still have the ability to go with the flow and not melt down when life delivers a curve-ball. The key here is to be goal-oriented and focused, but allow room for letting disappointing things happen without falling apart when the best laid plans go awry—because they will. Going with the flow is what happy people have as plan B.[19]

I must confess that I have rehearsed many speeches to give to certain women in my life, because I didn't get done for them what I had so hoped to accomplish. I have written far too many defensive emails and texts; and today I am sad that I wasn't secure enough in Papa God to take a deep breath, stop the rehearsal and simply say, "I am sorry." Only three words, without a novella of an explanation.

I want to share with you now another characteristic of controlling women that I am convinced has become worse in the past twenty years, not just among Evettes—this is a culture-wide pattern. This "unholy habit" is sort of like anxiety. It promises that the more we engage in it, the better we'll feel, when in fact, it intensifies our defensive condition.

WHINING: THE NATIVE TONGUE OF THE CONTROLLER

Now that you have this handy acronym, you can remember what happens to the controlling woman. She gets TIRED: Trapped. Irritable. Rigid and Resentful. Exhausted. Defensive. These are the results of pinning on your Junior God Badge and trying to become the Super-Omni Wannabe Deity. But here's ano,ther result that makes a slight alteration to our acronym and introduces a critical component to the profile of the controlling woman.

I was teaching this material in Arkansas, and when I said the term *tired*, it was pronounced by others as *tarred* (like "tarred and feathered"). I got a kick out of this, and then I also realized that substituting the letter *a* in the place of the *i* was actually perfect! The *a* represents *anger* in the life of the controlling woman. I know that many Christian women are very uncomfortable with the word *anger*, but the reality is this: Controlling women are often "tarred" and they are *angry* when life doesn't go their way. This is a state of mind that has its own native tongue—*whining*.

Whining is simply *anger* squeezed through a tiny hole. The moment you hear whining, you can tell that someone is angry that her demanding spirit has been stifled by a detour, or worse, a "no." Christians don't take whining seriously enough. We tend to see it as someone being just a little cranky. But the Old Testament does not rate whining as so harmless.

Let me tell you a story about when God first awakened me to my fluency in whining. Years ago I was scheduled to speak at a women's conference and the event was held out-side in 101-degree heat…and I was required to wear a long dress. The conference planners had put large fans on the platform so that the speakers and singers would not melt. As I stood singing, waiting to walk up to the platform, the sweat (yes, holy sweat) began to run down my body, and my head started to look as if someone had poured a bucket of water on me. I looked at the fans and plotted how to position myself directly in front of them when I began speaking. Looking forward to some cool air as I walked up on the platform, I was thrilled that the gusts of air were soon blowing right on me. It was fabulous. I launched into my message.

Suddenly, though, I noticed the women in the first row were beginning to move in their seats. It only took me a second to figure it out. I was sweating so profusely that the fan was sweeping my sweat onto the women in the first row. I apologized to the women being sprayed with my holy sweat and I stepped away from the fan for the rest of my talk. When I was finished, I rushed offstage, eager to change out of my sweat-drenched dress. However, I was told that the van was leaving for the airport immediately, and there was no time for me to change. The drive to the airport took more than an hour and, as you can imagine, I was sweating even more, crammed into a packed van. (I did feel sorry for those sitting by me.) The moment we arrived at the airport, I ran for the ladies' room.

As I peeled off my wet dress and started putting on dry clothes over wet undergarments, I became what I have since termed an "Egyptian-Delivered Whiner." It's probably a miracle I heard my flight announced, because of the cacophony of griping and whining in my head. After takeoff, I was looking out at the clouds and having a very lively interior fuss-fest. Just that morning, before the holy sweat tent meeting, I had read that clouds are flags to remind us of God's faithfulness. Gazing at the clouds, I began thinking that God is the ultimate sky-writer. All of a sudden, this thought came into my heart: "You want to fuss and complain? Then quit serving the King. Go and work at Burger King instead, Jackie. But don't pretend to serve the King again from this day forward with such whining and complaining." That simple thought stopped my whining dead in its tracks. I couldn't even conceive of the prospect of not being able to serve the *King*. It is the greatest joy and privilege of my life to tell people there's hope in Jesus no matter how much pain you've been through, no matter how crushed and broken you are.

It was a jarring moment. I immediately grabbed my Bible out of my purse and began to look up the Scriptures that confront the seriousness of whining. It's serious because God has delivered us, and like the ancient Israelites, to whine and complain after such glorious deliverance is an affront to Almighty God. God's chosen people were delivered from Egypt only to become Egyptian-Delivered Whiners. This was an intolerable behavior, because it insulted God's goodness. As I began to search for the Egyptian-Delivered Whiners in the book of Numbers, I found a massive chorus of them, singing in the key of C—that's C for *complaining*! (Num. 14:1-2).

Now, in these chapters the lead whiners were men, not women. Ten of the leading men were whining over what they could not control. Male or female; whining is an equal opportunity offender. Moses had selected twelve men (one from each tribe) to explore the land that God had promised His people. These men were to report back to Moses about the land and the people living in the land. There is a children's song that tells the story of the men sent to spy out Canaan, and the chorus states, "Ten were bad and two were good." In actuality, twelve good men were sent to spy in Canaan, but fear transformed ten of them into complaining whiners. Ten came back fearful and fussing. Two, Joshua and Caleb, came back believing God would give them what God had promised.

Here is something to keep in mind. The complaining men had a much more significant effect on the rest of the community than the great faith of Joshua and Caleb did. Whining and complaining are contagious. "And they spread among the Israelites a bad report about the land they had explored" (Num. 13:32). As it turned out, 2.4 million of the people aged 20 and above died in the wilderness and never entered the Promise Land. These people did not die because they were sexually immoral or drug dealers or embezzlers. No, *they died because they were angry whiners.*

Consider this moment whom your whining is impacting—spouse, child, friend, Bible study members? Just thinking about the contagion of whining made me nauseous. At that time in my life, I could've been president of the Palm Beach County Whiners Club.

The controlling woman has no idea that she whines incessantly, *because it is her native tongue*! Put another way, it's the water she swims in. When our daughter was young, she had a problem with whining—not a shock, considering that she was trained by the ultimate controller who spoke fluent whining daily. In true irony, I could see the whining as unacceptable in our daughter but couldn't see the "beam in my own eye" (see Matthew 7:3-5). When Jessi would whine, I would put my fingers in my ears and say, "I can't hear you when you whine." Well recently, I was on a whining binge, and suddenly my husband stood up and put her fingers in his ears and walked out of the living room. At first I burst out laughing, but then I remembered the seriousness of whining and I immediately stopped. I stood in the middle of our living room and examined my heart to locate the fuel line of anger and fear that had me whining so profusely. Talk about a sin that easily besets a controlling woman like me!

For years after the plane flight when I got my first whining tutorial from the book of Numbers, I focused exclusively on the whiners. At one point, though, I was preparing to teach on the seriousness of whining and decided to look a little more closely at the two men who did not join the whining chorus. Caleb was from the tribe of Judah, and *Judah* means, "Praise." When Caleb saw the enemy, his immediate reaction was praise God. Caleb responded in faith rather than in fear.

I used to get aggravated when I heard the phrase, "Praise the Lord anyway!" It always felt disingenuous to me. I thought it covered up reality by sugar-coating the situation or that the people who said it were in denial. But rereading Caleb's comments, I could see his worship and praise as the speech of faith: He was fluent in the language of praise: *Praise the Lord! I faced the enemy. I faced the giants. I faced the darkness. I faced the potential battle. And I can't wait to see what God is going to do with this suffering.* Because God never wastes suffering, He has the last word. Caleb didn't complain because he was declaring his faithful anticipation of what the Lord God was going to do. Worship is a boast that you can't constrain. "Then Caleb silenced the people before Moses and said, 'We should go up and take possession of the land, for we can certainly do it'" (Num. 13:30). "Because my servant Caleb has a different spirit and follows me *wholeheartedly*, I will bring him into the land he went to, and his descendants will inherit it" (Num. 14:24, emphasis added). When someone follows God *wholeheartedly*, whining is not a compatible behavior. Whenever I find myself whining, I know immediately that I am more focused on following my own script and agenda wholeheartedly than I am on following the script God has written for me.

The painful prospect of fighting giants in the Promised Land was not intimidating to Joshua, either. Joshua came from the tribe of Ephraim, the tribe known for being fearless fighters. Those from the spiritual tribe of Ephraim know that they have a choice to whine or a chance to worship like Caleb. Like Joshua they can look forward to what God will do with the pain. People can be fruitful in their suffering when they give their pain to God as material for sacrifice. Such a living sacrifice will be touched by God, and He can bring something beautiful out of something painful.

THE "TARRED," ANGRY CONTROLLER BURIED WITH MOSES

Controllers become angry when things do not go the way they planned. Controllers become frustrated when other people are upset, because they cannot fix what is wrong. I used to assume that my anger was just a manifestation of the sin that so easily trips me up—control. Then God used a chapter in the Book of Numbers to shed some new light on my aggravation and frustration with life.

Moses and Aaron were faced with an angry crowd (more than two million strong) that was upset by a life-threatening situation. There was no water for all of those people in the middle of the desert. The people wanted Moses and Aaron to tell them what they planned to do about the need. Moses and Aaron took this enormous need to God, who told them exactly what to do: "Speak to that rock before their eyes and it will pour out its water" (Num. 20:8).

As Moses and Aaron gathered the grumbling people in front of the rock, something happened. I believe that Moses moved from a position of faith in God to being angry with the complaining crowd. Instead of speaking to the rock, Moses struck the rock in anger (see Numbers 20:11). Moses' anger at the rebellious, grumbling people robbed him of the trust that he had demonstrated in the presence of the pharaoh and at the edge of the Red Sea. God saw Moses' anger with the people as a missed opportunity to honor Him in front of the people: "Because you did not trust in Me enough to honor Me as holy in the sight of the Israelites, you will not bring this community into the land I give them" (Num. 20:12).

That passage just breaks my heart, because I am sure that Moses knew what it was to trust, but he was blinded by his anger with the people. Instead of focusing on God and the rock, Moses took his eyes off the glory of God and focused on the murmuring community he was leading. The people's problem with trusting the God of Israel became Moses' problem. Think about this in your own life. Do you ever strike out verbally when things are out of control? I have never struck a rock or even a wall or a tire, but I have verbally struck out in a screeching whine when things are out of control.

For several years, whenever I would read about Moses' anger and the consequence (not entering the Promised Land) I would grieve that my anger, like that of Moses, could cost me the "promised land" (meaning my inheritance in Jesus, not heaven). I felt sorry for Moses, because it seemed that his frustration and anger with a rebellious group of people could be justified. After all, who wouldn't be frustrated with people who would still doubt after witnessing the parting of the Red Sea?

Then, however, God showed me that even Moses, man of great faith (see Hebrews 11:23-29), struggled with trusting God. His struggle was manifested through his anger; Moses' anger was a symptom of his lack of trust. I would never have correlated my anger with circumstances or people as a deeper root issue of not trusting in a sovereign God. Now whenever I am angry, I try to consider not only the person or circumstance, but the extent to which I am failing to trust God. I do not want my tombstone to be in "Moab." God did not permit Moses to enter the Promised Land; therefore, he was buried outside the Promised Land in Moab. (See Deuteronomy 34:1,5-6.)

Sadly, women who habitually wear Junior God Badges end up, more often than not, like Moses. *Moses got angry at the whiners.* He died because of his response to the behavior of other people. Controllers are angry most of the time because of the way other people act. Not uncommonly, I encounter women's ministry teams that are fussing and whining about the way others have dropped the ball with regard to things they were asked to do for the event. Controllers get angry because of what people did not get done, and also about the lack of gratefulness for all that the driven controller accomplished when she picked up the slack for those other women.

As I became more sensitive about my need to stop whining, I asked the Lord a very serious question: "How am I going change when I am surrounded by 'kindred whiners?'" He patiently reminded me that Joshua and

Caleb traveled in the wilderness for forty years with 2.4 million whiners, and they still made it to the Promised Land.

Are you tired of being tired? Are you longing for the issue of control to be constrained so that the chronic fatigue of control can subside? Are you ready to lay down the terrible burden of always having to have life under your control? In chapters 9 and 10 we will look at some concrete steps for recovering from all of this.

GOOD NEWS FOR THE TIRED, FRAZZLED, AND CHRONICALLY FATIGUED WOMAN

A gift for every Junior God Badge owner is the grace of God that allows our lives to count for him when we are running around like a crazy woman trying to get things done. When I look back on the pace of my life, I see so many times that I was a total mess. Then one day the Lord showed me something comforting: Even when I am frazzled, I can't smudge Him out of view! God used the bitter woman Naomi to show me this sweet gift of grace. "Don't call me Naomi, she responded. Instead, call me Mara (bitter), for the Almighty has made life very bitter for me" (Ruth 1:20 NLT).

Naomi was bitter because she had lost her husband and both of her sons. Yet this bitter woman caused her daughter-in-law Ruth, the young widow of one of her sons, to choose the God of Israel. This shows that God can use someone even during their darkest hours when faith has been outrun by pain and bitterness has taken over! Even bitterness can't hide God's light in you. Bitter Naomi was a witness to her widowed daughter-in-law, regardless of her sour state of mind, and Ruth chose the only true God over the gods of Moab:

> *Don't urge me to leave you or to turn back from you. Where you go I will go, and where you stay I will stay. Your people will be my people and your God my God. Where you die I will die, and there I will be buried. May the Lord deal with me, be it ever so severely, if even death separates you and me* (Ruth 1:16-17).

The treasure of Jesus inside the life of His followers is a presence so powerful and so bright that even a flawed believer cannot totally extinguish Jesus, the light of the world. Beth Moore validates this premise that I have shared for so many years: "Nothing brings me more relief than the absolute certainty that human hand prints can't smudge the face of God when He's bound and determined to reveal a glimpse of Himself." [20]

Reading that quote pumps me full of such giddy joy! On our worst day, you and I can't smudge out God's revelation of Himself through our lives. You may feel trapped, irritated, resentful, exhausted, or defensive—even angry—but all of that cannot mask the great treasure you contain in your soul. That makes me want to skip and whistle like a child on summer vacation. "We now have this light shining in our hearts, but we ourselves are like fragile clay jars containing this great treasure. This makes it clear that our great power is from God, not from ourselves" (2 Cor. 4:7, NLT).

DISCUSSION QUESTIONS

1. Do you find yourself irritated by an ever-expanding to-do list? Would your list exhaust the Proverbs 31 woman? Why do you think this is (or isn't) the case? (See Proverbs 31:10-31.)

2. Rigid vs. Flexible—which one describes you? How does it describe you? Remember: "The mature Christian is one who understands that life is more chaotic than predictable!" (See Numbers 9:17-22.)

3. How might you be viewed as the family nag? How do you feel about this? (See Proverbs 19:13; 21:9,19; 27:15-16.)

4. With reference to the exhaustion of the controlling woman, discuss this quote: "Many people commit to a 120% life and wonder why the burden feels so heavy. It is rare to see a life pre-schedule to only 80%, leaving a margin for responding to the unexpected God sends our way." (See Exodus 18:17-18; Luke 10:38-42.)

5. Are you too reachable? How might you have become the local "911"? Are you teaching people to go to the throne and not to the phone? (See Psalm 18:19; Isaiah 46:4; Hebrews 4:15-16.)

6. "Whining is the native tongue of controlling women." Examine the seriousness of whining. (See Numbers 11, 13, 14.) Would you be described as a woman who whines more than she worships? What does this indicate that you need to do?

CHAPTER 9

CONTROL AND LOVED ONES

On long road trips, my husband and I used to listen to Dr. Laura Schlessinger on the radio. She has been described as one of the most popular talk show hosts in radio history, and we enjoy (most of the time) her no-nonsense advice infused with a strong sense of ethics. Listening to The Dr. Laura Program, I noticed that at least 80 percent of the callers want advice for how to control or change someone they love. Whether the caller is a parent concerned for a rebellious child or a wife who is struggling with her husband or a sibling concerned about another sibling's very poor choices, they all moan and groan when they hear Dr. Laura's standard reply: "There is nothing you can do about another person—you can only make good choices yourself."

Ken and I learned to expect it. Whenever we would hear callers phrasing a question along the lines of "what can I do?" we started calling out the answer! We both knew that Dr. Laura would tell the person that they cannot change another person's character. Naturally, most callers would try to rephrase their questions in hope of getting a better reply (a reply that would tell them how to open the eyes of the blind).

This reminds me of what Donald Miller wrote: "One of the greatest breakthroughs I've experienced was realizing my relationships were designed to be enjoyed, not to be fixed."[21] This quote might be shocking for the wannabe deity who is still trying to hold on to her life's script of fixing others. The controlling woman we've been looking at throughout this book doesn't have time to *enjoy* the people in her life, because she is too busy trying to fix them. She has a messiah complex that must be crucified so that she will finally be able to surrender her Junior God Badge willingly! The Omni Super Woman is trying to fix everyone else—from her grandmother to the check-out clerk at Walmart, from the church administrator to her daughter's teacher—there is hardly a person beyond her scope of "helpful" and "necessary" adjustments.

In this chapter we will cover only a few of the lucky individuals she is trying to fix. And we will start with every woman's first control project—the man she loves. She will often defend that she is only trying to make Mr. Wonderful even *more wonderful*…but is she really?

CONTROLLING MR. WONDERFUL

When Ken and I were in Paris a few years ago for our thirtieth anniversary, we couldn't wait to visit the Louvre and the Musée d'Orsay. We so enjoyed looking at the masterpieces housed in these incredible museums, and I was excited to reach the part of the Musée d'Orsay where Monet's work is displayed. As I walked into the room where his famous painting of the lily pads is displayed, I was taken aback by what I saw. The painting was framed with much of the unfinished canvas displayed. Without thinking about why the unfinished canvas was displayed, Ken snapped a picture of me in front of the painting. After returning to the States, I started to assemble our pictures, and I came upon the Monet picture. As I looked at the unfinished canvas, the Lord whispered in my heart, "Jackie, the people that you love are like this unfinished masterpiece."

I thought about that for a while. I began to think about how ridiculous it would be if I were to carry my own brushes and paint into the museum in order to *finish the Monet*...you know, just touch up the edges. The French police would have me in handcuffs in a heartbeat, while my husband would have to try to explain why his wife was "touching up" a masterpiece. I realized that too often throughout my life I have tried to "touch up" the human masterpieces that are around me. My tendency to want to change those I love, and even those I know more casually, is like a vain attempt to paint the unfinished edges of other people's lives. Each one of us that knows Jesus is God's masterpiece, the work of His hands (see Ephesians 2:10). Only God has the right to touch up the masterpieces that He has begun. Now whenever I have the desire to change someone I love, I can hear God whispering, "Jackie, put down that paint brush!"

C.S. Lewis understood this masterpiece principle. He wrote, "We are...a Divine work of art, something that God is making, and therefore something with which He will not be satisfied until it has a certain character."[22] When I am tempted to touch up *any* masterpiece that I see, I will rest in the fact that God will finish His masterpieces at His pace and His pleasure and not mine. God's Word calls me to *admire* the masterpieces around me and allow the unfinished edges to be completed by His brushes and paint alone.

Sadly, women often miss the fact that in the list of the top five needs of every man is the word, *admiration*. My husband is changed more by my admiration than my many vain attempts to transform him. Have you been trying to touch up the masterpiece of your husband's life with your own paint and brushes? How often has a married woman been shocked and dismayed when some woman her husband works with captures his heart? How did she do it? Sometimes it was simply through admiration. Way too many men go to work and receive more admiration from the women they work with than the woman they come home to each day.

Controlling women can be too busy to add "admiring my husband" to their to-do list. If admiring your husband has not made your to-do list in some time, then write the title of this book on your list and buy it as soon as you can: *Love & Respect,* by Dr. Emerson Eggerich. As a recovering Junior God Badge wearer, that book has so blessed my marriage. The book helped me to see clearly that I am too busy emasculating my husband through control that I never have creative energy left for one of his greatest needs—respect and admiration.

Oh, and while I am discussing your husband's needs, I just want to remind you that his greatest need is sex. Why would I mention that in a book on control? Well, because the chronically exhausted, controlling woman does not have the energy for sex with her husband. And God's Word is very clear about the danger of neglecting your man's greatest need (see 1 Corinthians 7:5).

In First Samuel 25, there is a story about a wise and beautiful women named Abigail who was married to a man named Nabal who must have been very difficult to put up with. She was an intelligent and beautiful woman, but her husband was called a "fool," and he was surly and mean in his dealings (see 1 Samuel 25:3).

This story of a wise woman married to a fool of a man captured my heart in the middle of the night some twenty years ago when I couldn't sleep, because I was grieving for a friend whose foolish husband had broken her heart. A habit of mine when I can't sleep is to get up and read my Bible. This particular night when I opened my Bible, I came upon First Samuel 25 and read the amazing story of Abigail. God used her story to show me how a woman can do what God wants her to do, even when married to a fool. I was so inspired by Abigail's wise choices that I began writing a message titled: "How to Be a Spirit-Controlled Woman Even When Married to a *Fool*." Some people might read the title of the message and think that Abigail was not being respectful of her husband, but in fact, Abigail simply was not in denial about the man she was married to. Here is where Abigail spoke with the future king of Israel about a very poor choice her husband made: "Please pay no attention, my lord, to that wicked man Nabal. He is just like his name—his names means Fool, and folly goes with him" (1 Sam. 25:25).

I have met so many women who will defend their husbands' foolish choices and do their best to create an image of their husbands that will impress others—until those people spend some time with him. Controlling women think that they are the defense attorneys for their husbands. These same women will use what they *can't control* in their husband's lives as an excuse to not do what God has planned for their lives. As a result, the controlling woman ends up being controlled by the fool she is vainly trying to control.

Whenever I get to know a woman who is in a difficult marriage, I immediately invite her to study First Samuel 25. Abigail did what was right without using her husband as an excuse. She appealed to David as a mediator and did not passively accept the fact that he would have killed her husband and all the men on their property if she kept silent. Some women, who have misunderstood biblical submission, would call Abigail's bold choice of standing as a mediator between David's fury and her husband's foolishness unsubmissive. Or one might see Abigail as controlling. Yet the biblical account expounds on the *wisdom* of her choice, including encouraging the future king of Israel:

> *David said to Abigail, "Praise be to the Lord, the God Israel, who has sent you today to meet me. May you be blessed for your good judgment for keeping me from bloodshed this day and from avenging myself with my own hands. Otherwise, as surely as the Lord, the God Israel, lives, who has kept me from harming you, if you had not come quickly to meet me, not one male belonging to Nabal would have been left alive by daybreak"* (1 Sam. 25:32-34).

Although Abigail's husband was a fool, her wise behavior saved the lives of all the men who worked for her husband (her husband, if you keep reading the story, died of natural causes). In Hebrew the name Abigail means, "A father's joy." I believe that Abigail brought God joy when she acted wisely, especially in the context of being married to a fool. However, if you examine the tables of contents of books written about women of the Bible, you will notice that Abigail is often excluded.

I believe Abigail is the classic example of how to handle a foolish husband. I have a friend who speaks at women's events, and she is married to a Nabal-like husband. This woman's faithfulness to God is not contingent upon her husband being wise, loving, or kind. Like Abigail, my friend knows how to walk in the joy of doing the very thing she was created for and not allow her circumstances or her husband to keep her from being fruitful. She has learned how to thrive and not just survive.

Throughout the past four decades, I have met many women who are crazy about Jesus even though their husbands are either spiritually apathetic or even modern Nabals. Many women are married to men who are more passionate about their hobbies than they are about Jesus. Twenty-five years ago, a wonderful friend named Sandy started an amazing ministry to women who are in marriages where the husband and wife are not compatible spiritually. The ministry is called "WAR," which would seem like a fitting description of a challenging marriage, yet WAR stands for the opposite: WAR stands for "Women at Rest." This ministry encourages women to be wise and courageous like Abigail even when their husbands do not share their passion for spiritual things. These women have learned how to let go of the longing to control their husbands' walks with the Lord.

So how does a woman control a fool? *She doesn't!* However, with God's help, she can control her choice to make the kingdom of God her primary concern and she can leave her hubby and family on God's transformation list.

A woman named Jeannette Texidor wrote the following personal account:

In my walk with the Lord I had such an amazing gift that I felt it was my job/duty to bring my husband at the time to salvation. I left around books, videos, tracts, anything I thought would reach him. We had a rough five years of marriage, an "unequally yoked" marriage. As a baby Christian I did not heed the Word's warning about being unequally yoked and was living a nightmare as I grew more and more in love with the Lord and farther and farther away from my spouse who wanted very little, if nothing, to do with God and all He offered. I tried everything I could imagine, manipulating situations and people to try to bring him to knowledge and understanding of what I had found. I would at times be a poor witness by losing my temper and arguing about the grace of God....

My attempts to control his heart and manipulate his mind never worked, and it was a rude awakening for me, albeit a good lesson on the fact that God is God and I am not.... What a blessing to have learned to trust Him and see what He can do that I could never accomplish.... I try to pick up my badge from time to time, but now I know better. I let Him take control of my life and those in it.

CONTROL'S GREATEST CHALLENGE—PARENTING

All mothers on this earth seem to face this struggle daily: the struggle to shape their children into good people. They invest hours and money and holy sweat to influence the direction of their children's lives. They invest more in their children than anything else in their lives—and then they are often very surprised when their children don't make good choices.

My husband made a choice before he even became a father—that he would break the legacy of sadness that came from his father, who was largely absent because of his absorption in business. His father equated working so much with loving his family. He valued his work more than relationships. My husband wanted to be a super father, and I was the happy partner in such a passionate goal. My dysfunctional family left me starved for a loving family, as well. I, too, wanted to be a good parent—in contrast to my life experience with dysfunctional parents.

I have shared a lot in this book about my experiences as a parent. I loved my kids passionately and we had a blast as a family. But I was also the queen bee of helicopter mamas and had to learn that there were painful consequences from all my hovering. What I want to tell you now is a story about how this overbearing mom had a sobering wake-up call in June of 1996. How can I remember a moment that long ago? Well, when a young person points out a big flaw in your life and you write what she said on Post-It notes all over your house—it's not hard to remember!

I was invited to speak at Second Baptist Houston at a singles' event. The young, single woman running the event was named Jody Hatt (now Maxwell). She was full of joy and passion for Jesus, and I was looking forward to our lunch together after the event was finished. As I began eating, Jody asked me if she could share something with me. My reply was, "Of course!" Little did I know that one of the biggest corrections in my life as a mom was going to come through this vivacious single gal; she was about to deliver a "punch to my gut." She said that when she was younger (which is funny because she was only 24) she and her brother made a decision that when they graduated, they would move seven states away from their overbearing mom. Wow. How could their mother be so overbearing that they would want to flee like that? Was she cruel? Was she abusive? Was she an alcoholic or enmeshed in some sick lifestyle? No. Jody told me that her mom was so passionate for Christ that she was determined Jody and her brother would be just as passionate, and her hovering and pushing was all meant to achieve that end. That comment captured my heart and I stopped eating.

Jody continued on to tell me that when she and her brother first arrived in Texas, having escaped the blades of mom's Junior God helicopter, they did not go toward things that would please the Lord. But then, after two years of living outside the Christian box of good behavior, Jody's brother said to her one night as they were walking out of a bar, "So are you done with this crazy lifestyle?" And Jody said, "I sure am." They chose to go to a big local singles' group at Second Baptist Houston, where they became involved and began to grow into passionate lovers of Jesus. Jody explained that they now look forward to seeing their passionate-lover-of-Jesus mom and sharing with her all that God is doing.

This story was challenging to my heart, and I thought she was finished. But I saw her take a breath, and she proceeded to deliver the final blow to my soul. Jody said, "You have made some comments about your concern for your son, and this is what I want you to know. His struggle… *it's not about you, Mrs. Kendall!* It is about his relationship with Jesus and not his relationship with his passionate mom." That simple phrase, *It's not about you, Mrs. Kendall,* was branded into my soul that day by the Holy Spirit. When I got home, I wrote it on many Post-it notes and put them up all over my room to remind me: *It's not about you, Mrs. Kendall.* I am forever grateful to Jody Hatt Maxwell for loving me enough as a sister in Jesus to share the painful truth of my being an overbearing mom. My passionate control had blinded me. I failed to understand that wanting to control the spiritual temperature of my children trespasses in God's territory. (For more details about being an overbearing, "OB"mom, you can read my book *The Mentoring Mom.*) Fittingly, about a year after this loving confrontation, someone sent me a banner with the following words written on it: "Do not feel totally and personally responsible for everything. That's *My* job. Signed, God."

LIBERATING THE CONTROL FREAK MAMA

Some years ago the Lord gave my daughter Jessica something in her devotions that has had a lasting impact on me. Jessica was studying John 17 when she came upon verse 17, which reads, "Sanctify them by the truth, Your Word is truth."

Jessica looked up the Greek words for *sanctify*, and she found a definition that thrilled her: "God is the ultimate agent of causation."[23] "To cause" is defined in Webster's dictionary as "to effect by command, authority, or force."

For the woman who longs to be completely delivered from her Evette addiction to control, this definition is very liberating. The sanctification of a life is the result of God's glorious "causation" in a person's heart—not my causation or yours. *Jehovah-mekoddishkem* is a name for God that means "the Lord who sanctifies you"[24] (Exodus 31:13), and it is *His* "authority, command and force" that causes change. Grasping this truth has altered what I pray for people. Now I pray that God will sanctify them "through and through" (see 1 Thessalonians 5:23), and then I can release the outcome of my longings, because I know Who the agent of causation is—*God, not me.*

This is the same principle Jody exhorted me with: "It is not about you, but God." That young woman understood that God is the ultimate agent of causation. He alone changes the human heart. And what does God use to sanctify people? *His Word*...not His Women. If you love someone whose heart needs changing, just keep asking *Jehovah-mekoddishkem* to sanctify them through and through. I can return to the Lord's daily assignments with joy and confidence in the ultimate agent of causation: *El Elyon*, the Most High God, the only sovereign.

The agent of causation is "large and in charge"! He will finish the work that was once begun. Some kids start out really strong spiritually, and then they go through a time of struggle, doubt, and disillusionment. Such a time of struggle can be very hard for a parent to witness. You may be wondering, "What is happening to my child?" You need to remember that the start is the promise of the finish: "Being confident of this thing that He who has begun this good work will perform it till the day of Christ Jesus" (Phil.1:6, NKJV).

This means that when your child makes a bad choice, you need to remove your Junior God Badge so you will not be tempted to fix the mistake or block the consequences. The natural consequences for bad behaviors are great instructors! I remember crying in the shower one time asking God how to treat this child of ours who had made a bad choice. Do you know the reply I heard deep in my soul? "Treat him exactly as you treated him yesterday!" (Which is to say, that I am to love my child unconditionally—before and after bad choices.) The Junior God Badge wearer will often overreact to a child's poor choice, and the overreaction is so shaming that the shame can do more damage than whatever the kid did in the first place. *We are called to love our children as they are and pray for where they need to go.*

PARENTING ADULT CHILDREN: CONTROL IS IMPROBABLE AND DESTRUCTIVE

I have a wonderful friend who is the mother of six adult children. We were having lunch one day when she made a remark that caused me to burst out laughing. My friend has the kindest heart and the sweetest voice, so when this sentence came out of her mouth, I almost couldn't contain myself. We were discussing the challenges of parenting adult children when she said, "I have come to the conclusion that the best way to parent adult children is to *shut up*. That is life-impacting wisdom for any parent of an adult child. If you have not learned this invaluable piece of wisdom and you continue to try and control your adult children, you will eventually not have a relationship with your adult children.

Even if your adult child asks your opinion or advice, I advise you to proceed with caution. I have always been too quick to reply to any question, and my adult children have been a great tutorial in being *slow to speak* and *quick to listen* (see James 1:19). Of the many parents I know who think they are still in charge of their adult children, I have observed how many times these children have moved far away!

Our two children, who were close to each other growing up have, interestingly, adopted different parenting styles. Different doesn't mean one is wrong, it just means different. From the beginning of mankind, free will has been a God-given gift, and Ken and I are learning how to respect the parameters of choices made by our adult children. Many of our kids' choices are reflective of their upbringing, but several of their choices are new to us. We have read up on what they are doing, and we have again decided to respect their wisdom and right to choose their hearts' direction for their own children without consulting us. I was reading an interview of a young movie star who is the age of our daughter, and she was being asked about being a new mom. She remarked about the joys of motherhood, but she also remarked about all the "unsolicited advice" she is constantly receiving. I grinned when I read her remark, because I thought to myself, "She is hearing from adults who haven't learned the deep lesson of not giving advice unless asked."

Ken and I have several friends who, like us, only contribute when asked. Several of us as parents of adult children have taken the free time we now have and are prayerfully looking for opportunities to teach, mentor, and advise young couples who are hungry for wisdom and insight that they did not grow up with and who could use some input. The local church is constantly looking for mentors for younger couples. Therefore, instead of driving your grown kids crazy in your attempts to control them as adults, take all of your hard-earned wisdom and pour it into hungry couples who really need *and want* direction for their marriage and their parenting journey. Too often we are trying to feed those who are not hungry and we ignore the starving young people around us.

NO TRESPASSING

Years ago another speaker and I were discussing the difficulty of influencing our families of origin. We admitted to each other that people all over the United States wanted to hear us speak, but our own families...well, that would be another whole book. This speaker mentioned something new she was learning about all people. She said, "People's hearts have barbed wire around them and a sign that says NO TRESPASSING." That was more than thirty years ago, and I have never forgotten it. Controlling women have cuts all over their bodies because of trying so many times to climb over that barbed wire fencing! I have used up many boxes of Band-Aids because of the bleeding emotional cuts from such foolish attempts. As with our husbands and children, when it comes to our original families, *only God* can change a person's heart (see Jeremiah 17:8).

In my Bible study recently, women were discussing children who are not as close to Jesus as they had hoped they would be. As we shared with one another our concerns and how burdened we were for each child, I had a new thought. I said to my friends, "We need to put our kids on a heart transplant list." We all know we cannot change our child's heart (whether young or old), so we need to put them on a "transplant list" by faith and then begin waiting with hope for the arrival of a new heart. This is the exact same thing we need to do with our parents and siblings, even our cousins, aunts, uncles, and grandparents. While you wait and you're tempted to put your hands on your hips with one foot tapping impatiently, remember, you are waiting for the *Lord*. So, whenever your heart is aching for change in the life of someone you love, just thank the Lord for the heart transplant list that Ezekiel effectively described (see Ezekiel 36:26-27).

DIFFICULT RELATIVES

As I wrote above, I could personally write another whole book on this issue of trouble with difficult family members. I have witnessed the painful impact of dysfunctional family members not only in my life but in the lives of thousands that I have ministered to during the past four decades. While reading *Smart Girls Think Twice,* by Jan Silvious, I came upon a definition of the difference between *relatives* and *family.* Jan's explanation has helped me to navigate more effectively the rough waters of difficult family members. I think the following quote will help you when dealing with toxic family members:

> Family is a safe, connected group that leaves you emotionally intact and even enhances your life. Relatives are those to whom you are linked by history, but you do not share with them a sense of community and connection. Your job is to be gracious, but you don't have to keep trying to make something happen that neither of you wants.[25]

You may want to read that quote again and then write it in the front of your Bible. That quote helped me remove my Junior God Badge in relation to trying to "make" relatives safe to be around and accepting that often my true "family" will consist of the God-fearing friends I choose in this life—my "forever family"!

When discussing the wannabe omnipresent woman in chapter 4, I introduced the concept of a "ministry of absence." It's worth revisiting here, because, honestly, it is such a foreign concept to the tribe of wannabe deities. When my friend first told me about this idea, I asked her to clarify her remark, because in more than four decades of walking with Jesus, I had never heard this expression. She calmly implied that when I listen to the same drama over and over again, my listening is a by-product of delusional hope based in denial. This wise mentor knows that I have spent years listening to dysfunctional drama from my family of origin as well as from my "forever family." She said it was time for me to enter into this ministry of absence and leave room for the heavenly Counselor to deal more intimately with my friends. The Scripture I shared earlier is worth repeating: "Nevertheless, I am telling you the truth. It is *for your benefit* that I go away, because if I don't go away the Counselor will not come to you. If I go, I will send Him to you" (John 16:7, HCSB).

In the context of loving God best by loving people well, God used my friend to show me that I need to get out of the way—be absent for a while—so the incomparable heavenly Counselor could lead my dear friends into a deeper dependency on Jesus and His Word. It is too easy for us to depend on our godly friend—sometimes holding onto that friend more tightly than Jesus. Years ago I heard Beth Moore warn a large audience of women of the danger of clinging more tightly to their best friends than to Jesus. She suggested that each woman place the cross between herself and her BFF and that both women hold on to the cross rather than each other.

My friend Ruthie sent me this excerpt from the writings of Henry Nouwen that describes this ministry of absence:

> If it is true that ministers are the living memories of Jesus Christ then they must search for ways in which not only their presence but their absence reminds people of their Lord. This has some concrete implications. It calls for the art of leaving, for the ability to be articulately absent, and most of all for creative withdrawal…. We have to learn to leave so that the Spirit can come. Then we can indeed be remembered as a living witness of God…. When our absence from people means a special presence to God, then that absence becomes a sustaining presence. Jesus continually left his disciples to enter into prayer with the Father.[26]

A DELUSIONAL HOPE JUNKIE

The suggestion of creative withdrawal was a refreshing revelation to this exhausted, controlling woman who did not want to appear uncaring, unloving, unsympathetic. But I also realized that to ask a controlling woman to let go, pull away, and enter into a time of absence could be seen as unloving, if not absurd. The Junior God Badge wearer prides herself in always being available to encourage her friends. But here's the irony. Far too often that encouragement is just the thing that equips someone with the stamina to continue in her drama! As an additional help, I was given a book to read titled, *Necessary Endings*, by Dr. Henry Cloud. In the fifth chapter I came upon a quote that made me realize the craziness of my delusional attempts to keep doing the same thing again and again, while expecting different results. Here is Dr. Cloud's sobering remark that exposed my wishful thinking. I called my wishful thinking "hope," but it was actually grounded in denial and delusional desire:

> Hope is designed to give us more time, so that whatever we are hoping for can come to pass. But because that is what hope does for us—buys more time and spends it—it sometimes creates problems if we are not in touch with reality. In that case, it is hope that keeps us going down a road that has *no realistic chance of being the right road* or making what we want come to pass. In a false reality, hope is the worst quality you can have.[27] (Emphasis added)

I have often referred to myself as a "Hope Junkie," because I believe that in Jesus there is fathomless hope. I have spent years writing an "anti-doubt" journal that fortifies my strong attachment to the hope that is in Jesus. What I have been learning as I am being weaned from my Junior God Badge is that my hope must rest in Jesus—alone. Hope does not lie in my capacity to change another person's drama by being her "Prozac" in the moment of crisis. That is not *hope*—that is me listening and being sympathetic so that a friend or family member or coworker can continue in the wishful denial of the reality that is her life.

In applying the ministry of absence, I mentioned specific things for my needy friend to do (find a counselor and support group) and I told her that I would check back with her in a month. Rather than our talking and texting regularly, I would be praying more and talking less. I actually did this with a couple of women, and they have gotten counselors and attended support groups. In the meantime, my Junior God Badge remains in a drawer as I allow the heavenly Counselor do His deepest work in these dear sisters in Jesus. If you find that you are experiencing compassion fatigue, it may be that you need to take a leave of absence from ministering to a person or two in your life.

THE MAMA MOSES PRINCIPLE

Let's take a look at a woman from the Bible who, frankly, does not get much attention in Bible studies or sermons. I am speaking of the mother of Moses, Jochebed. I have been inspired by a principle that she exemplified, and I want to pass it along to you. It is a principle I gleaned from a book I mentioned above, *Smart Girls Think Twice*, by Jan Silvious. Even if you don't know much about Moses' mama, take note of this. She was a woman of such faith that she made it into God's "Hall of Faith." (See Hebrews 11:23.) What is the Mama Moses Principle? It is the principle that allowed a mama, Jochebed, to make a little floating cradle for her beautiful three-month-old son, place him in this ark, and set him afloat on the Nile River. Now,

I have been to Egypt, and in case you don't already know, the Nile is not a stream, but a big river.

The Mama Moses Principle is when a woman does everything she can and then, by faith, releases the outcome to God. For Jochebed, this principle kicked in when the pharaoh issued an edict to kill all Hebrew baby boys. So, Moses' mama hid her beautiful son for three months. When Jochebed could hide him no longer, she made a choice to do all she could: Build an ark and set her son on a journey of faith. Jochebed placed her little baby in the ark she built and set him on the great Nile River—*with no guarantee.* She had no idea what the outcome would be. Her son could have been rescued by a princess, eaten by a crocodile, or capsized and drowned by a rough current. Jochebed did all she could do and then released the outcome to God by faith. In fact, Jochebed gave Moses up to God twice: First in the floating ark and then to the arms of a princess.

The Mama Moses Principle allows you and me to do our best and trust God with the results. Daily, you and I can do our best as spouses, parents, friends, employees, employers—and then trust God with the outcome. With all our strenuous efforts, we need to keep in mind that the only guarantee we have is the grace to trust God when the ark is rocking and ready to capsize.

Twenty-two years ago, I was speaking at a conference in Hilton Head, N.C. where John Trent was one of the main speakers. I made sure that I got to his session early so I could sit down front. John Trent along with Gary

Smalley had written a best-selling book titled, *The Blessing*. My husband and I had both read the book and grasped the significance of a child receiving a blessing from his or her father. Blessings contain hope and affirmation and a declaration of unconditional love and acceptance, and these are components that every child needs. My husband followed the plan in the book and took our son away on his 13th birthday weekend. The book encourages fathers to write out special blessings to ask God to give their sons. God gave Ken a special verse to pray over Ben that weekend, and Ken had the verse framed for Ben to take wherever he would go in the future: "About Benjamin he said: "Let the beloved of the Lord rest secure in Him, for He shields him all day long, and the one the Lord loves rests between his shoulders" (Deut. 33:12).

You can imagine how excited I was to sit under this man who had so inspired Ken and me as parents. As John began to teach about the blessing, he spent a lot of time expounding on the blessing that Father God gives us, even when our earthly father never gives us a blessing. I sat there, grateful all over again for the extravagant blessings I have received from my heavenly Papa God. My earthly father never gave me a blessing; instead he gave me a heart wound that took years to heal.

John went on to share his own personal story about flying to see his dying dad and longing and hoping for even *one word of affirmation* from his dad—one small kindness. John then said something that pierced my heart so that I began to weep. John said, "Do you know what my father said to me during the eight hours I was by his bed? He spent eight hours telling me what a loser I was."

Can you imagine how crushed John must have been? With that kind of "anti-blessing," how is it that John is not bitter himself? Yet, he is not. In fact, John Trent has an amazing ministry that is focused on *encouraging* his brothers and sisters in Jesus. John did not get earthly affirmation from his father, but the affirmation and love he has received from God through Jesus, has allowed something beautiful to grow out of something painful.

I have met countless adults who are desperate— even as adults—for their parents' approval. I have seen competent men suffocated by the lack of affirmation from their earthly father or mother. I know a man who made it to the Baseball Hall of Fame and yet has spent his entire life listening to his dad's comments about how he could have played a better game! *Really?*

The following is a letter that I wrote to a woman who was actually at that same conference. She had spent too many years, too many tears, too much over-thinking, trying to please an "unpleasable" parent:

Dear Friend:

You are so precious, and Jesus wants you to *stop trying to please* an "unpleasable" woman. Jesus wants you to sink deep into His love and acceptance. You have spent too many years walking on eggshells around your mama and it is time to remove your Junior God Badge and admit that your mama is never going to change. Your mom's identity is totally defined by her perfectionism. Your mama has not only suffocated you, but even her grandkids. Enough already. Are you ready finally for a change? Here goes:

Admit that your mom is not going to change, *but you can*. How can you stop this cycle of mama madness? I want you to Google the program Celebrate Recovery and take your precious self to the meetings. Join the breakout groups for codependent women who are eggshell walkers and enablers of every kind of addiction; and trust me—perfectionism is *not* a holy habit.

One of my sweetest friends is going to this awesome recovery group, and she is learning so much about *letting go of what others think about her*. You can actually learn how to end the Mama Drama! I remember learning years ago that addiction is the result of shame. And where does most of our shame begin—rejection from someone very significant—in other words, the lack of blessing and the lack of appropriate blessings from Papa God. You are now old enough to learn how to *let go* of your mom's opinion and embrace with the tightest squeeze Jesus' acceptance of your precious, adorable self!

Love from a fan, Jackie.

MAMA DRAMA

You may have been blessed with two affirming parents, and you need to hit the ground in worship right now for this amazing gift that you may have taken for granted. I was standing next to an amazing woman who is a best-selling author when she took a call. Within seconds, she was weeping. I had to wait for her to get off the call so that I could hear what tragic information had caused her to burst into tears. When the call ended, I learned that it was "mama drama" right there in baggage claim. This remarkable woman had been trying to share the most incredible experience of a lifetime, a blessing beyond measure. She had been as giddy as a child on Christmas, and her mom's response had been so negative and demeaning. This beautiful, competent lover of Jesus was incapacitated with pain from her mom's critical remarks, because she was still, at fifty years of age, trying to get from her mom what her mom is not capable of giving! She so wanted her mom's blessing, just as John Trent so longed to hear affirmation from his dad. Right there in the airport I instructed my friend to stop calling her mom for what her mom will *never give her*—affirmation. This gifted woman has lived half a century and is still trying to control the probability of a blessing from mama, but the probability is zero. That day I gave her a copy of my book on forgiveness to help her *let go, move on, and forgive* her mama's madness.

Unfortunately, many controlling women still believe deep in their souls that they can eventually change their parents' heart attitude from criticism to affirmation. When the controlling woman learns how to remove her Junior God Badge, she will find herself more consistently focused on God's marvelous blessings and not be held captive by a critical remark from a spouse, a child, a parent, a friend, or anyone else who is breathing on this planet. Is this possible? *Yes!* I am a woman who used to be held captive by any criticism, or even perceived criticism, from the mouth of someone I love. Now I consider the source, I consider the truth that the criticism may contain, and then I return to Papa's lap, where I am reminded of this verse: "I am unworthy of all the kindness and faithfulness You have shown Your servant" (Gen. 32:10).

DISCUSSION QUESTIONS

1. How do you think you may have spent too much time trying to control Mr. Wonderful? (See Ephesians 5:33.)

2. How do you think you might have tried to make your children into your image of success? (See Psalm 139:14,16.)

3. How have you "wasted too many brain cells" trying to change your friends? (See Proverbs 17:17; 27:6.)

4. How do you think you may have been delusional about your power to change your adult child? (See Ephesians 6:4.)

5. Are you wasting one moment of your limited day pass trying *still* to gain the approval of your parents? How does this manifest itself in your life? (See Mark 10: 29-30.)

6. Who only can change the heart of a human being? Who alone is the ultimate "agent of causation?" Where does that leave us as competent people? (See John 17:17.)

7. Which of the above relationships is the hardest one to relinquish control of? Husband? Children? Friends? Adult children? Remember—ultimately such control is an impulse toward idolatry.

Chapter 10

CURE FOR THE CURSE OF CONTROL: REHAB FOR THE RECOVERING CONTROL FREAK

I wanted to end this book with some concrete solutions, a *cure* for the curse of controlling. Even though I have tried to offer some concrete recommendations throughout the book, that's the specific focus as we end our time together on these pages. This rehab program is presented in six steps, but first I want to share the primary reason any of us should want to recover from our controlling ways.

Just recently Papa God gave me fresh motivation to remove my Junior God Badge and surrender with reckless abandon to His script and abandon my passionate blueprints. There are so many things we miss while being so controlling (such as peace, love, joy, and more), but probably the greatest loss from being so controlling is the possibility of *missing Jesus*.

What do I mean by "missing Jesus?" Let me explain. One morning early, while reading God's Word, this particular passage just jumped off the page and captured my attention in a special way for the rest of the day:

> *The women who had come with Jesus from Galilee followed Joseph [of Arimathea] and saw the tomb and how his body was laid in it. Then they went home and prepared spices and perfumes. But they rested on the Sabbath in obedience to the commandment* (Luke 23:55-56).

Here we have these courageous women who remained at the foot of the cross along with only one of the apostles, John. These women did not run away in fear of what might happen to them. These women had been part of the "Gospel travel team" with Jesus, and they were totally faithful, even in a very dark moment. They watched the lover of their souls die. It doesn't get any braver than that. The women had followed Joseph of Arimathea to see where the body of their Savior would be put to rest. Once the women knew where Jesus' body was laid, they went home to prepare the appropriate anointing spices and perfumes. Now, all this may seem like very ordinary and predictable behavior, but verse 56 just grabbed my heart: "But they rested on the Sabbath in obedience to the commandment."

Here we have passionate lovers of Jesus who were not only loyal to Him, they were also grieving. This was a completely unique situation. Once their preparation of the spices and perfumes was complete, wouldn't you expect them to bolt out the door to take care of their precious Savior's body? These women had traveled with Grace Personified in the person of Jesus, so they knew that it was sometimes okay to violate the law for a greater good. Why didn't these women just assume that the end would justify the means in this situation? I put myself into this scenario, and let me tell you, I would be running to the tomb with the spices rather than worrying about the law. I would take charge of the situation; I would justify that love trumps law. The controlling woman always has a separate set of rules she has made up that justifies her controlling tendencies.

As I pondered this, my living Savior drew my attention to what a controlling Jackie would have encountered if she had run quickly to the tomb rather than waiting to honor the Sabbath first. If I had run straight to the tomb, I would have encountered a heavy stone that I could not have moved and a Roman solider who would have been harsh and threatening to me. What would this controlling woman have missed by running so fast rather than patiently waiting to do what was right? The women who obediently kept the Sabbath were utterly blessed when they went to the tomb. They did not have to roll back a big stone. They encountered an angelic messenger; and one of them had the glorious privilege of being the first person to see the risen Savior (see John 20:11-18). Mary Magdalene saw the risen Savior and then ran and told His apostles.

She had submitted to God's Sabbath script, and her wise choice resulted in incomparable blessing.

I pondered this passage throughout the day. Tears flowed as I considered the times I had missed seeing Jesus at work in this world because I was too busy running along on my scripted agenda—defending my wisdom against the unfathomable wisdom of God! Once I heard Pastor Justin Perry in Tampa quoting John Piper, and here is the great quote he used:

> It is a very arrogant and ungrateful [child] who has no keen interest in the goal that lies most heavy on his father's heart. The faithful [child] longs to know and understand his father's deepest intentions so that he can bring his thoughts and affections and actions into alignment with it.[28]

The controlling woman is so busy with her daily agenda that she often will miss the opportunity to consider the intentions of the Father's heart for the situations she finds herself in.

SIX STEPS FOR RECOVERY FROM BEING A CONTROL FREAK

Step 1: Ask God's Forgiveness for Putting His Crown on your Head

When I allow people to rely on me more than they rely on God, I have put God's crown on my head. When I make myself responsible for the happiness of others, again

I am crowning myself with God's crown. This crowning of myself is, at root, an impulse to idolatry. I may not ever be an "American Idol," but in the past I have been my family and friends' idol. I have been the go-to girl for whatever you need done. Now, however, the only crown I want on my head is a graceful garland of wisdom (see Proverbs 4:7-9).

Something that helped me in relation to keeping God's crown off my head was learning the names of God. Why did this help? The more I learned about God's incomparable capacity in *every area* of life, the more I could keep the crown on God's head rather than dare try to put it on mine. For years I taught about the names of God, and His names became like wallpaper on my soul and guardrails around my heart. When this control freak was tempted to put on her Junior God Badge and charge into battle—I would suddenly remember one of the precious names of God, and it would be a like a governor on my gas pedal to slow me down.

When someone I loved was in trouble, instead of immediately wondering what I could do, I would pause and match the need with a Hebrew name of God. Focusing on a specific name, I would praise God for what His Name reflected of His capacity. And do you know what I would notice? Peace began to take the place of anxiety. For example, when I would be tempted to try to fix one of my family members or a close friend, I would praise Jehovah-mekoddishkem, who alone changes the human heart! Or, if I felt alone in my struggle, I would stop and praise Jehovah-shammah, the Lord Who is There, right in the middle of my struggle. I could write a book on all the occasions that the names of God helped this control freak to take a breath, let go, and let God have His way.

A wonderful friend (Janet Falkman) wrote a poem that captured the names of God and what each one meant. God gave her this poem while sitting in a hospital waiting room. She was praying through a list that I sent her of my favorite names of God, and this was the impressive embellishment of that list that she was inspired to pen:

I praise You Elohim,
For You made me body, mind and soul,
I praise You El Elyon,
For You are in control.
I worship You El Roi,
For You see my every need.
El Shaddai I rest upon Your breast,
On Your comfort, I do feed.
Adonai I bow before Thee;
What You ask, that I will do.
Halleluiah Lord Jehovah,
There is no God but You.
I thank You Jehovah-rapha,
For the healing You do bring.
Jehovah-nissi, You are my Banner;
My protection in everything.
Praise You Jehovah-mekoddishkem,
For Your sanctifying grace.
I thank You Jehovah-shalom,

Your peace is found, seeking Your Face.
I thank You Jehovah-jireh,
For I know You will provide.
I rest in You Jehovah-sabaoth,
For You are on my side.
Jehovah-raah, You are my shepherd.
You are everything I need.
Praise You Jehovah-tsidkenu,
My righteousness is only in You.
Oh Jehovah-shammah I thank You,
That You are always there.
No matter how heavy the burden,
Your presence lifts my despair.[29]

We had a guest one summer who was such a blessing that her visit seemed much too short. During hours of sharing heart to heart, I told her about a new message I was developing entitled "Glory Robbers." I explained that, although we were created to bring God glory, we constantly rob Him of the glory He is due. Too many Christians have made their lives so "me-centric" that they rob His glory on a daily basis. After our wonderful guest left, she pondered the "Glory Robber" theme, and she sent the following message:

Being a glory robber is like being a bridesmaid who is more worried about making herself look good than making sure the bride and groom look good and have all they need. I was a bridesmaid back in May; I watched all of the other bridesmaids getting ready and worrying about how *they* looked and such. I just kept thinking, "No one is even going to be looking at us; we are delusional if at any point in this wedding we think it is about *us* as bridesmaids." It ticked me off when the bridesmaids were really only conveniently available when the photographers or videographers were around, but they were nowhere to be seen when it was time to take down the reception hall or unload trucks back at home. Glory robbers often serve the Bride of Christ and the Groom when it is convenient for them, or publicity is involved. "…everyone who is called by My name, whom I created for My glory… (Isa. 43:7).

The controlling woman can often act like the delusional, me-centric bridesmaids in the story. May we resist the temptation to be "ovation-aholics" and strive instead to be true servants of the King. Such servants are comfortable with esteeming others as more important than themselves (see Philippians 2:3). We controlling women tend to crave applause and affirmation, and we need to be aware of this blind spot. Let's look at another step toward recovering from being so controlling.

Step 2: Ask God's Forgiveness for Self-reliance and Pride in Your Own Capacity

This is the ultimate life verse of the woman who understands the need to surrender her Junior God Badge:

> *Lord, my heart is not proud;*
> *my eyes are not haughty.*

> *I don't concern myself with matters too great*
> *or too awesome for me to grasp.*
> *Instead, I have calmed and quieted myself,*
> *Like a weaned child who no longer cries for its*
> *mother's milk.*
> *Yes, like a weaned child is my soul within me*
> (Ps. 131:1-2, NLT).

The word *haughty* in the first verse of this passage refers to a "lofty arrogance and pride." Just think about lofty arrogance and pride. You might never consider those qualities to refer to your heart or your life agenda, but honestly, the Junior God Badge wearer moves with the arrogance of self-sufficiency, power, wisdom, and insight that begins and ends with *her*. Too many of us greet each day with much sufficiency and gusto—ready to offer our services to help God out in the world. Isaiah had some stern words about this:

> *Who among you fears the Lord and obeys the word of his servant? Let the One who walks in the dark, who has no light, trust in the name of the Lord and rely on their God. But now, all you who light fires and provide yourselves with flaming torches, go, walk in the light of your fires and of the torches you have set ablaze. This is what you shall receive from my hand: you will lie down in torment* (Isa. 50:10-11).

I have lived long enough to have watched countless women scrounging around for firewood to make torches for the lives of their struggling loved ones, rather than letting them become desperate enough to find the Lord. The irony of controlling is that we actually help escort our dependents to a "bed of torment"! All our efforts do not heal the struggling loved one; instead all too often we lure them away from the very situation that would compel them to turn to God. Controlling women would rather rescue the prodigal son *before* he has a chance to come to his senses in the pig pen. (See Luke 15:11-32.) She's the one who's sending care packages to the pig pen!

The self-appointed Superwoman can have a hard time recognizing that she's being self-reliant or full of pride. So, if you have decided to identify yourself with this tribe, simply assume it is part of your make-up. Ask the Lord to help you see how and when these tendencies manifest themselves; and then, as He graciously highlights your motives and actions, repent. In faith you can then receive God's forgiveness and His instructions, which may well include some of the following steps. These are the particular ways He has shown me to proceed when I repent of my unholy, characteristic habits of control.

Step 3: Resist Being an Egyptian-Delivered Whiner

In chapter 8 I wrote about *whining* being the native tongue of the controlling woman. As I began teaching about control at women's conferences, the Lord gave me a great word that helped me curb my own whining. This one word helped usher me more quickly into a grateful, worshipful lifestyle far away from the debilitating whiner lifestyle.

What is this great word? It is simply "whatever." Now, I know it's idiomatic in our culture and we're inclined to hear it as a sarcastic statement (think of a smirking fourteen-year-old saying "*what*-ever!") But this is a sanctified "whatever," and it allows a woman to remove her Junior God Badge and surrender to the script of a loving God. I first picked up on the importance of this word when reading a passage in a modern paraphrase of the Bible, the New Living Translation (and I'd like to point out that it was coming from the mouth of a teenage girl!): "For nothing is impossible with God. Mary responded, 'I am the Lord's servant, and I am willing to accept whatever he wants'" (Luke 1:37-38, NLT, emphasis added). Do you see how this works?

Let's think about Mary for just a moment. Here you have a sweet teenage girl who had just been told by a big angel that she was going to be impregnated through the Holy Ghost and that the incorruptible seed of Jesus Christ was going to grow in her womb. Talk about stunned—she was confused and disturbed—but before she could even express her doubts, the angel Gabriel reminded her of her cousin Elizabeth, who was carrying a miracle baby in her old age. God in His gracious kindness directed Mary's attention to another woman who was a little farther along in her miracle. All of us need the encouragement of a woman who is a little further along in her miracle, because it lends us hope about our own miracle, or the One we are longing for. After Gabriel mentioned Elizabeth, Mary could not restrain her response. Bursting out of her mouth came her holy "whatever."

Since I latched onto this word "whatever" in 2001, I have become convinced that every miracle is preceded by a "holy whatever"—a most humble and beautiful moment of surrender. The next time you find your perfectly curated life under assault, remove your Junior God Badge and whisper, "whatever, Lord." I am telling you, that whisper of surrender will keep you from becoming an Egyptian-Delivered Whiner.

From the moment I began teaching women how to move *from whining to whatever* and from there to worship (see 1 Thessalonians 5:18), I have been presented with watches, clocks, mugs, plaques, tee shirts, and pillows with the word WHATEVER emblazoned on them! Right behind me in my den is a door hanger that says reads, "Whatever," and in my quiet time room there is an animal print door hanger with "Whatever" printed on it. I appreciate all the reminders!

I have had many chances to practice this principle in my ongoing effort to resist complaining and whining, but a time in Richmond, Virginia was one of the earliest memories of actually resisting whining and being determined to worship no matter what the cost emotionally and physically. My sister-in-law and I were in Richmond for a women's conference, and we returned to the hotel *beyond tired*. We were dragging our suitcases and some boxes of my books with us. As we entered the hotel, we saw a huge crowd of young people. We were trying to move around them when we saw what the holdup was. It was prom night, and hundreds of teens were waiting for elevators—that had stopped working. DeDe and I looked at each other and realized how we were going to have to get up to our room—the stairs.

As we first started climbing the stairs, we were laughing at how crazy the juxtaposition of events was. DeDe suggested that this was a chance to apply all that I had just taught at the women's event. As we conquered the first several flights of stairs, we were able to resist being whiners, but as we dragged our suitcases up the stairs— twenty-four flights—you can imagine that they got heavier and heavier. We were beginning to lose our resolve to resist being whining women. We started to ask Jesus out loud for the strength to persevere and not be cranky by the time we arrived at our room. We kept saying, "We want to be worshippers, not whiners!" Every time we passed another floor number, one of us would say out loud something to be grateful for. When we got to the twenty-fourth floor, huffing and puffing, we came out of the stairwell and both started laughing. Our hearts were full of genuine joy, all because we had intentionally resisted being complaining whiners.

Please remember this: When you're whining, your little joy tank gets punctured. Whining drains you. A controlling woman *thinks* her boss, her church, her kids, or her husband drains her. But, no, the reality is that whining about your boss, your church, or your family drains you! It's all-important to practice intentionally catching whining in its tracks and putting a stop to complaining with the power of praise! As I mentioned in chapter 8, I don't think most Christians see whining as sin; most see whining as being simply human. True enough, but much of our humanness is sin! Recently, when preparing to teach on the "Dangers of Whining," I revisited a familiar passage about whining:

> *Do everything without grumbling [whining] and arguing, so that you may be blameless and pure, children of God who are faultless in a crooked and perverted generation, among whom you shine like stars in the world* (Phil. 2:14-15, HCSB).

These verses expose the reality that when I am whining, I am not shining. Notice, as well, that the verse also mentions *arguing*. This passage tells us how to be blameless and pure and shining in this dark world. The primary sins to avoid? Not drugs, adultery, greed, but *whining* and *arguing!*

In the children's song, "This Little Light of Mine," there is a stanza that addresses not letting satan blow our light out. Well, I would like to state the obvious: We extinguish our lights more than satan ever does—through our whining and complaining. You know what I mean; when life clashes with my terms, I end up not only whining, but also becoming agitated and argumentative with those who are blocking me from reaching my self-established goal.

James wrote about this. Maybe the next time you get aggravated with someone who kept you from crossing the finish line of your noble to-do list, you will remember this verse: "What causes fights and quarrels among you?

Don't they come from your desires that battle within you?" (James 4:1). This must be a human problem that is not new for today's Christians, because these lines were written to early Christians, whose internal battles boiled over into external ones. Oh, the pleasure of finishing my to-do list, and oh, the anger that I feel when someone cramps my style and seems to be blocking my dreams. Most controlling women assume that God is going to give them the desires of their hearts—their dreams. After all, doesn't the Word tell us this? "Take delight in the Lord, and He will give you the desires of your heart" (Ps. 37:4).

However, the bottleneck stems from a misunderstanding of the word "delight." In Hebrew, *delight* refers to something being "soft and pliable."[30] Controlling women are rarely capable of taking delight in the Lord because, far from being soft and pliable, they are too busy manipulating and maneuvering the people in their universe. Wearing their Junior God Badges, they are more likely to be angry and fretting, a behavior that is reproved in these verses: "Refrain from anger and turn from wrath; do not fret—it leads only to evil" (Ps. 37:8).

Not that the controlling woman sees herself as angry or fretting. How can a little fussing be sinful? The word *fret* doesn't refer to anything "little," though. It means to "kindle and burn with anger." God is warning us that our anger is a dangerous place to live and that being soft and pliable (taking delight in Him) is the best way to cure that fretfulness. Anger and fretfulness lead only to evil, not to healthy desires and dreams. Yet the controlling woman is easily angered when she perceives that an "evil" person is succeeding when she is not. Her frustration increases with the success of those around her when she perceives that she isn't getting her desires and dreams.

After struggling for so many years with anger and making harsh remarks, I finally began to understand the correlation between my angry remarks and an "ailing" (sick) heart. I found a verse in the book of Job referring to the anger that flows from an ailing heart (see Job 16:3). I looked up *ailing* in Hebrew, and it means "to be vehement, to irritate, pressed."[31] Talk about a searchlight being turned on in my soul! I began to understand that my controlling propensity is a major source of my own anger. I began to admit that my heart had filing cabinets full of records of frustration and irritation with people and circumstances that I cannot control. All of these have been pressing on my heart, and the overflow has irritation—and vehement anger at times. By God's grace, I now see that my whining is just anger squeezed through a tiny hole, and this particular whiner has been a very angry woman with issues that I have ruminated over for years. Through forgiving many people, my ailing heart is getting better, and my angry mouth and argumentative attitude are becoming more of a distant memory than a daily occurrence.

The next time you are with an argumentative, controlling woman, pray for insight into the things that have been pressing on her heart and causing such an angry overflow. The next time *you* are that woman, ask the Lord to reveal what *really* ails you. The past does not excuse our present anger, but it can give us valuable clues to deal with the unresolved issues that are fueling an angry, argumentative attitude. Pray to know what areas of your ailing heart may harbor fermenting storage tanks, so that you can safely empty them before they spill out through angry lips.

I must bring up one more aspect of the danger of anger in the life of the controlling woman: The controlling woman is not only ignoring God's script, she is actually grieving the Holy Spirit. A controlling woman can remain angry for days, which shuts down the influence of God's Holy Spirit dwelling within her. The Word is clear about this: "Do not grieve the Holy Ghost of God, with whom you were sealed.... Get rid of all bitterness, rage and anger, brawling and slander, along with every form of malice" (Eph. 4:30-31).

When I do not rid myself of anger's control, I forfeit the Spirit's control. What an extravagant waste to live a life that is controlled more by fermenting anger rather than the precious Spirit of God. The whining woman throws water on the fire of the Holy Spirit and quenches it.

One last thought: When I was in my early thirties, I was probably one of the angriest women on two feet. I was exhausted by my anger and I whined incessantly. I used to wonder how I had *any* friends, I was so unpleasant to be with. Then I suddenly realized something: Most of my friends were whiners too, so they were entirely comfortable with my angry, complaint-filled demeanor. It simply mirrored their lives. At least we woke up to what we were like. By God's grace, my friends and I have grown so much since we were in our early thirties. It's not that we aren't tempted to whine from time to time, but we are much more likely to choose worship over whining at this more mature time in our lives. Praise be to God! At last we have learned this truth: *When I whine, I don't shine.*

Step 4: Guard Your Heart and Mind Against Fear

Last year I got a belated Christmas gift that came in the form of a visit of a young woman who is in seminary. I knew the Lord had something special for our time together, because it worked out to be squeezed into such a tiny window of free time for both of us. The Lord always teaches me something during our times together. Courtney is the young woman who translated the verse I used at the beginning of this book (see Genesis 3:16).

She and I were returning from errands together when I was explaining something to her and I happened to quote Second Timothy 1:7, at which Courtney responded, "Can I have an index card? I want to share with you the amazing treasures that are hidden in that verse!" I ran to my den to get an index card before unpacking my grocery bags. As I was putting things away, Courtney sat at the counter and began writing. As she began to explain what she wrote on the card, I knew that Jesus was giving this gift, not only to me but to every woman who would read this book. I could have included this insight in the chapter on fear, but I knew that I wanted to give you one more soul care gift as you complete this book, so I saved the best for last.

I have quoted this verse thousands of times because I prayed it over our daughter every night of her life as a little girl, but I never had known the insights into its meaning that Courtney shared with me: "For God hath not given us the spirit of fear; but of power and of love and of a sound mind" (2 Tim. 1:7, KJV).

The first thing Courtney explained to me is this particular word *fear* comes from the word *delias* from which we get the word "delirious." She explained that word for disorienting fear—panic—is used only here in this verse and in the two passages about how the disciples panicked on the stormy lake and how Peter panicked as he walked on the water to Jesus in the storm (see Matthew 8:26 and Mark 4:40). The panic that the disciples experienced was a disorienting fear. (I am comforted knowing that even men have their delirious moments of fear.)

On the index card, Courtney wrote down a variety of fears—phobia, trauma, and terror. Yet the idea of "spirit of fear" being "delusional" thinking kept me up for hours pondering its application. I could think of so many situations when I overreacted to bad news and began to speak and act deliriously. I have heard countless women speaking this "delirious" language when they were afraid of the outcome of a trial they were facing. How quickly we can fall apart in disorienting fear!

I know there is a remedy, though. The moment I hear my own delirious comments or catch myself in delirious self-talk, I can expect a gift from God. I assumed Courtney was going to share that God gives us a sound mind in contrast to delirious, delusional thinking. Now, I wasn't wrong, but I learned that it was even richer than I had imagined. "Sound mind" comes from two Greek words, *sophroneo* and *phrono*. Sophroneo refers to a healthy mind, and it means *shalom*. Shalom is one of the best words ever, meaning salvation, peace, well-being, and so forth. *Phrono* refers to the frontal, executive part of the brain, where our decision-making takes place. In other words the delirious mind and the mind of shalom are connected, because in place of our delirious self-talk, God has given you and me the capacity to have His *shalom* in the frontal, executive lobes of our brains—which is to say, the "peace of God, which surpasses all understanding" (Phil. 4:7 NKJV).

Courtney explained that the gift that replaces the "spirit of fear" is a "sound mind," which denotes profound peace, as in: "He will not fear bad news; his heart is confident, trusting in the Lord" (Ps. 112:7, HCSB).

The moment you or I receive bad news or foresee potential disaster in the life of someone we love, instead of moving immediately into delirious, fearful thinking, we can place our hand on our forehead and take a moment to praise Jehovah-shalom for the peace of God that is readily available in this moment:

> *Be anxious for nothing, but in everything by prayer and supplication, with thanksgiving, let your requests be made known to God; and the peace of God, which surpasses all understanding, will guard your hearts and minds through Christ Jesus* (Phil. 4:6-7, NKJV).

This works! The other day when I got bad news, I cried for several minutes, and then I began to move into fearful thinking about my future. Immediately, the Lord brought Second Timothy 1:7 to my mind, and I remembered that I have a choice: To yield to delusional thinking or to look to God for shalom in the thinking part of my brain. I sat on the stairs drying my tears and choosing to praise God for shalom in the executive part of my brain. As I thanked Him for the peace, He graciously reminded me what He had showed me that very morning in my quiet time—that I had nothing to fear because He was my "exceeding great reward": "Do not be afraid, Abram. I am your shield, your exceedingly great reward" (Gen. 15:1, NKJV).

Delirious fear compels a woman to start running in several different directions to try to fix something that appears to be broken. This woman will spends hours frantically researching what can be done. So many brain cells are wasted on what is not real, but rather delusional.

I honestly wish I had understood the depth of this passage of Scripture before then. I had spent more than four decades grappling with this delirious fear in myself and in other women, young and old. I did my best to speak hope into my heart and theirs, but I would have loved to have been able to share this powerful verse so that fearful ranting could cease in that moment. I didn't know it could be so simple: Delirious fear. Pause. Place hand on forehead. Whisper, "Jehovah-shalom I need You to be my peace." Profound peace.

We controlling women have tried to do this on our own. We can use our energy to resist delirious thinking. Now we know what to do! Even if we may be delirious for a few moments, we don't have to build a condo there. As soon as we recognize what state we're moving into, we simply *stop* and *pray*. We surrender those disoriented, fearful thoughts to God. He will make the exchange: switching out the madness for transcendent soundness of mind.

Step 5: Learn to Sail Instead of Rowing So Hard

I was running on the treadmill and listening to a sermon when a very elderly minister said he wanted to share his greatest regret with the audience. I almost stopped running, because I didn't want to miss a single word this older man had to share. (I have learned that God wants to teach us much through the older ones in our life—the ones who are still experiencing miracles of hope.)

I was anxiously anticipating an amazing revelation from this older man, but he shared the simplest sentence. He said, "I wish I had learned to sail sooner in ministry rather than rowing so hard." I immediately thought of the way I have rowed so hard against the wind rather than hoisting a sail and yielding the boat of my life to the wind of God's Spirit—blowing my life wherever He wanted. This is a hallmark of control, we row *against* the wind rather than surrendering to the wind of God's Spirit. Upon registering that old minister's comment, I began to picture myself rising in the morning, hoisting the sail of my life, and looking forward to where the wind of God's will would take me. Even if some days the wind doesn't come, leaving me just sitting still, then I can leave the oars alone and simply wait for the wind. God says, "Be still, and know that I am God; I will be exalted among the nations, I will be exalted in the earth" (Ps. 46:10).

Of course I know that for controllers, the word "wait" is like a cuss word.

But if you are a recovering controller who has removed her Junior God Badge, you can actually accept the reality that sometimes *being still* is a great, God-exalting moment. How is being still ever very productive in the scheme of life's demands? It is productive silence because the stillness has to do with ceasing to worry and allowing the "Commander of a million stars" to handle the complex outcome of the challenges in your life. Being still—in faith—actually accomplishes more than all of our running and fretting and manipulating. If you remove your Junior God Badge, you will be able to be still enough to hear and brave enough *to do* what the Most High God desires. This is learning to sail rather than row. This will enhance your capacity to live with a surrendered spirit, flexible and strong to face a life that is predictably chaotic.

I have a dear friend who totally understands this concept, and we often joke that the wind of God's Spirit seems to direct our "boats" to the opposite sides of the lake, over and over. No matter how often we try to turn our sails so that we can meet up on the same side of the lake, we miss each other on a regular basis. Life has us on the opposite sides of the lake, but we can end up smiling every time because we have learned to rest in the One whose Spirit blows on the sails of our little skiffs!

Step 6: Have the Faith to Remove Your Junior God Badge

Now that you have read the previous chapters, I hope you have thought of certain activities from which you need to take early retirement. You have probably considered some areas of your life where you need to say "no" more often than "yes." As an older woman, I want to encourage you to say "no" as much as you need to, but *never* to say "no" to your time with Jesus.

For too many years I have heard people say that we no longer need to be "under the law" that requires daily quiet times with the Lord. Not only have I heard this in casual conversation, I have also heard it preached from pulpits and broadcast on Christian radio. I always wince when I hear such a remark. Why would anybody want to cut off their source of life and strength?

Walking consistently in the principles that I have shared in this book requires an enormous amount of faith. A recovering Head Chick in Charge needs daily infusions of faith in order to allow God to continue to run the universe and to humbly accept whatever God has in His script for her each day. I *know.* As a woman whose greatest desire is to stop being so controlling, I know the amount of faith such a change requires. I also know, from forty-eight years of personal experience, that faith cannot be purchased online or at Walmart or even Nordstrom. Faith has only one way of entering our hearts. How? Through time in God's Word. Busy, controlling women are always trying to explain why they don't have time in the day for a holy intermission with God. Yet there is nothing further from the facts!

Forty years ago when I got married, our college offered a summer seminar elective titled, "Women and Fulfillment." I was a newlywed, so I was anxious to learn from the older woman who would be teaching the course. Her name was M.E. Cravens, and she was one of the most beloved teachers/counselors on our campus of four thousand students. Little did I know when I signed up for the seminar that I would learn something that would impact me for the rest of my life. (In fact, seven of the eight books I have written contain the truth I learned in this seminar.)

On the first day of class, Mrs. Cravens introduced a "show and tell" opportunity. Yes, a show and tell—I know it was college and not elementary school, but the effect of the assignment was profound. A clipboard was passed around to every woman in the seminar to fill out her name and the day she would present something that brought her fulfillment. I was thrilled that I was the last woman to sign up for this presentation. Why was I thrilled? Mrs. Cravens explained that each woman was to bring something from home to demonstrate what brings her fulfillment in life, and I knew that the first thing that had come to my mind could cause a little disturbance among the women in the room.

Day after day I watch these short show and tell presentations, all the while thinking about how I would present what I would bring from home. Some of the presentations I remember: One woman brought mason jars that she had filled with homemade jellies; another woman brought all of her knitting projects; one woman brought some needle-point; yet another brought canvas with some paint. As I was leaving the seminar one day, the teacher said to me, "I can't wait to see your show and tell." Somehow I knew she already knew what I would be bringing to class.

My turn came. I picked up my Bible and put it in a brown bag. My hesitation about bringing my Bible to class as the representation of my greatest fulfillment was the fear that the other women in the class would think I was trying to display my spirituality like a Pharisee would. I was young, and my people-pleasing problem was causing me undue stress as I walked into the seminar. When Mrs. Cravens asked me to come and show the class what I had brought, she stopped me in my tracks as I began to pull my Bible out of the grocery bag. She said to the women in the seminar, "I already know what is in Jackie's bag." I had tears in my eyes, and when I looked at Mrs. Cravens, she also had tears in her eyes. What she said to the class in the next few minutes changed my life forever. (I had been in two previous counseling seminars with her, and through my remarks she had gotten a glimpse of the importance God's Word to my soul care.)

She stood in front of the class holding my Bible, and she said, "Jackie has learned at a very young age what has taken me fifty-six years to learn. She has already grasped that *there is no lasting fulfillment, happiness, or success in life without a consistent, daily, growing relationship with God through His Word."* Mrs. Cravens expounded on this statement for the rest of the class period. She talked about how long it took her to realize that no matter what keeps her hands and mind busy, it would never bring lasting fulfillment without the holy intermission of daily time spent with Jesus in His Word.

That was years ago, and I have never stopped. Along the way I found a method of Bible study that has helped me—and thousands of others—be consistent without having to neglect the lengthy to-do list. For more than two decades, I have used *The One Year Bible. The One Year Bible* offers a daily format that helps me be consistent. All of us are busy and easily distracted by daily activities and I find that having a simple structured plan helps greatly.

Every day's reading is divided into four parts: Old Testament, New Testament, Psalms, and Proverbs. These bite-sized increments are not too long or complex, and with four sections, you've got four chances to get something meaningful out of your "face time" with God.

Honestly, if you don't get anything out of the Word, why would you read the Word? This does not mean that every day brings a profound revelation, but if we are not attentive daily to God's love letter, the Bible, we minimize our chances of catching onto His ways of showing love to us. I have taught professional athletes to use this easy method because, trust me, they have the hardest time concentrating when they read. But these bite-sized pieces of God's nourishment keep anyone from gagging on the discipline of daily reading.

Groups of women all over the United States exist for the sole purpose of encouraging each other to take care of their soul daily by getting some time with Jesus in the Word. There are large groups on Facebook, such as "Sisters in the Word" and "Yada Yada Sisters in the Word." I recommend adopting a method such as this, and finding encouragement to continue. It will bear abundant fruit in your life.

Early one morning, my granddaughter, who was visiting, found me in my room having my quiet time and she said, "What are you doing, Mimi?"

I replied, "What does it look like, sweet girl?"

Emma said, "You are reading the Bible." And I added, "Emma, Mimi is having her spiritual breakfast! Mimi's soul needs breakfast every day!"

She looked at me intensely for a moment and then sweetly said, "I love you Mimi!" That moment with Emma Grace was "yummy" spiritually and emotionally!

Times with God ensure that we will be "tuned in" to Him. We will recognize his voice when we hear it, and we will learn to obey. As the Word says, "These instructions are not empty words—*they are your life*" (Deut. 32:47, NLT, emphasis added). Here's a story that illustrates this perfectly:

In June of 1996, I heard Steven Spielberg being interviewed about his work with Holocaust survivors. He brought out a woman named Gerta, one of the few women who survived the Death March during World War II. The march went from Poland to Czechoslovakia; it was three hundred miles and three months long.

Gerta told an astounding story. She recounted that one afternoon in the concentration camp in Poland, she was told that all the women were going on a walk. Just before leaving, her father called to her across the courtyard and yelled, "Gerta, put on your boots!" It was June, and all the young girls were barefoot, including Gerta. But, being a good Jewish girl, she knew not to argue with Papa. So there was Gerta, putting on boots in June to take a walk, assuming, of course, she would return to camp.

This obedient young woman survived what turned out to be a three-month ordeal, because she listened to her Papa. She watched the other girls breaking off their toes like twigs as their feet froze at night. Gerta watched hundreds die from their feet upward—as she survived in her boots.

What an extraordinary story of the simplest, yet most profound provision by God. Gerta's story is a challenge to all of "Papa's" children (see Galatians 4:6). Our heavenly Father knows the march we are on, and He alone knows what is ahead for each of us. So when He gives us instruction—even when it doesn't make sense (see Isaiah 55:8-9)—we need to listen to Papa.

This swift obedience is certainly part of our reckless abandon to Him. *Surrender your Junior God Badge* and live with intentional focus on God's list for your day rather than your own list. By faith, give God a blank sheet of paper with your signature at the bottom. This blank sheet with your signature is your heart's permission for God to draw up the blueprints of your life. By listening to Papa, you can take early retirement from being responsible for the happiness of everyone in your life!

A PRAYER OF SURRENDER FOR THE CONTROLLING WOMAN

Lord I ask Your forgiveness for the days I have spent whining and griping about my lot in life when You have blessed me beyond words. Lord, forgive me for insulting Your goodness when I whine and argue with You concerning my agenda. Lord, forgive me for snoopervising, for anger, for directing rather than surrendering—and all such faithless behavior. Forgive my neglect of time with You. May I from this day forward go without eating or brushing my teeth before I neglect my time in Your Word. Forgive me most of all for being so busy that I can't hear the whisper and songs of Your exceeding great love for me. May I be handcuffed to the Holy One, so I will know Emmanuel's agenda for the days ahead, in Jesus Name, Amen.

DISCUSSION QUESTIONS

1. Share a specific area in your life where you may be controlling.

2. How do you think you might have become an idol in someone's life?

3. How are too many people in your life more dependent on you than God? Which ones depend on you too much and what can you do about it?

4. What would keep you from surrendering your Junior God Badge?

5. Are you like Gerta when it comes to obeying your heavenly Papa? Or are you like too many of God's children, who would argue about wearing the boots and probably start marching without the Father's guidance?

6. Are you ready to surrender your Junior God Badge? Are you ready to retire from being a wannabe omnipresent, omnipotent, omniscient, sovereign, Jehovah-Shalom deity?

7. Write your own prayer of surrender (include the date).

Date: _____

ENDNOTES

1. Jackie Kendall, *Say Goodbye to Shame* (Shippensburg, PA: Destiny Image, 2004), 78.

2. Suzy Toronto, *The Sacred Sisterhood Of Wonderful Wacky Women* (http://www.goodreads.com/work /quotes/2044080-the-sacred-sisterhood-of-wonderful -wacky-women).

3. Jessica Wuerffel, wife of Heisman Winner Danny Wuerffel.

4. Donald Miller, "How to Know if You're a Controlling Person" *Storyline* (blog), January 20, 2014, (http://storylineblog.com/2014/01/20/how-to-know-if -youre-a-controlling-person/).

5. Jackie Kendall, *A Man Worth Waiting For* (New York: FaithWords, 2008), 218.

6. Old Testament Lexical Aid, 10198, Strong's #H9592.

7. Beth Moore, *To Live is Christ: The Life and Ministry of Paul* (Nashville: Lifeway, 1997).

8. Taken from *Blue Shoes* [book on tape], Anne Lamott, River Books, 2002.

9. Adapted from Jackie Kendall, *Free Yourself to Love* (Nashville: Faith Word, 2009), 186–187.

10. Interview with Bill Hybels, "The Secret of Strategic Neglect," *Leadership Journal* 37:1 (Winter, 2015), 31.

11. Letter of C.S. Lewis to Arthur Greeves, 20 December 1943. In *The Quotable Lewis* (Wheaton, Ill: Tyndale, 1989), 335.

12. Les Parrott III, *The Control Freak* (Wheaton, Ill: Tyndale, 2000).

13. Paul Trip, "Wednesday's Word," blog, Feb. 20, 2013 (http://www.paultripp.com/wednesdays-word/posts/worship-god-as-sovereign#.USUsNvJzRy0.email).

14. Nancy Guthrie, *Holding on to Hope* (Wheaton, Ill.: Tyndale, 2002), 26–27.

15. Jerry Bridges, *31 Days Toward Trusting God* (Colorado Springs, Colo.: NavPress, 2013), 17.

16. Oswald Chambers, "Gracious Uncertainty," April 29, *My Utmost for His Highest* (Grand Rapids, Mich.: Discovery House, 1992).

17. Richard A. Swenson *A Minute of Margin* (Colorado Springs: NavPress, 2003), Lesson 53.

18. Swenson, Lesson 66.

19. Tamara Star, "7 Habits of Chronically Unhappy People," *The Huffington Post*, posted 11/18/14, updated 12/29/14. (http://www.huffingtonpost .com/tamara-star/7-habit-of-chronically-unhappy -people_b_6174000.html).

20. Beth Moore, *So Long, Insecurity: You've Been a Bad Friend to Us* (Carol Stream, Ill.: Tyndale, 2010), 342.

21. Donald Miller, Facebook post. August 25, 2013. (www.facebook.com/permalink.php?id=71430761720 &story_fbid=10151555984316721)

22. C.S. Lewis, *The Problem of Pain*, as found *in The Complete C.S. Lewis* (Grand Rapids, Mich.: Zondervan, 2007), 571.

23. *Hagiazo, Key Word Study Bible*, N.T. Lexical Aids (Chattanooga, Tenn.: AMG Publishers, 1996),1572.

24. Chris Poblete, "The Names of God: Jehovah Mekoddishkem," *The BLB Blog*, posted August 14, 2012 (http://blogs.blueletterbible.org/blb/2012 /08/14/3926/)

25. Jan Silvious, *Smart Girls Think Twice* (Nashville, Tenn.: Thomas Nelson, 2007), 112.

26. Henri Nouwen, *The Living Reminder: Service and Prayer in Memory of Jesus* (New York: HarperCollins, 1977), 50.

27. Dr. Henry Cloud, *Necessary Endings* (New York: HarperCollins, 2010), 85.

28. John Piper, "The Glory of God as the Goal of History," *Desiring God* archives, October 12, 1976 (http://www.desiringgod.org/articles/the-glory-of -god-as-the-goal-of-history).

29. Janet Falkmann, April 5, 2000.

30. James Strong, *Strong's Exhaustive Concordance* (McLean, Va.: MacDonald Publishing Company, 1980), #6026.

31. Strong's #4834.

ABOUT THE AUTHOR

Jackie Kendall is President of Power to Grow Ministries. She is a National conference speaker and the best-selling author of Lady in Waiting, The Mentoring Mom, A Man Worth Waiting For, Free Yourself to Love: The Liberating Power of Forgiveness, and Waiting for Your Prince. She has been married 41 years to Ken and they have two married children and three grandchildren.

For speaking engagements or to get more information, contact Jackie at:

Power to Grow Ministries, Inc.

www.jackiekendall.com